Previously Published Wellek Library Lectures

The Breaking of the Vessels
Harold Bloom

In the Tracks of Historical Materialism
Perry Anderson

Forms of Attention
Frank Kermode

Memoires for Paul de Man
Jacques Derrida

The Ethics of Reading
J. Hillis Miller

Peregrinations: Law, Form, Event
Jean-François Lyotard

Reopening of Closure: Organicism Against Itself
Murray Krieger

Musical Elaborations
Edward W. Said

Three Steps on the Ladder of Writing
Hélène Cixous

Other Works by Fredric Jameson

Sartre: The Origins of a Style
Marxism and Form: Twentieth-Century Dialectical Theories of Literature
The Prison-House of Language
Fables of Aggression: Wyndham Lewis—The Modernist as Fascist
The Political Unconscious
The Ideologies of Theory: Essays, 1971–1986, 2 vols.
Late Marxism: Adorno; or, The Persistence of the Dialectic
Signatures of the Visible
Postmodernism; or, The Cultural Logic of Late Capitalism
The Geopolitical Aesthetic; or, Cinema and Space in the World System

Fredric Jameson

THE SEEDS OF TIME

*The Wellek
Library Lectures
at the
University of
California, Irvine*

COLUMBIA UNIVERSITY PRESS

NEW YORK

COLUMBIA UNIVERSITY PRESS

NEW YORK
CHICHESTER, WEST SUSSEX

Copyright © 1994 Columbia University Press

Library of Congress Cataloging-in-Publication Data

Jameson, Fredric.

The seeds of time / Fredric Jameson.

p.   cm. — (The Wellek Library lectures at the University of California, Irvine)

Includes bibliographical references and index.

ISBN 0-231-08058-1

1. Postmodernism (Literature)   2. Utopias in literature.

I. Title.   II. Series.

PN98.P67J36   1994

809'.93372—dc20   94-8735

                                                       CIP

Casebound editions of Columbia University Press books are printed on permanent and durable acid-free paper.

Printed in the United States of America

c 10 9 8 7 6 5 4 3 2 1

The Wellek Library Lectures in Critical
Theory are given annually at the University of
California, Irvine, under the auspices of the
Critical Theory Institute. The following
lectures were given in April 1991.

The Critical Theory Institute
John Carlos Rowe, Director

for Wang Feng-zhen

. . . for who can look into the seeds of time

And say which grain will grow and which will not . . .

Contents

Introduction   *xi*

PART ONE   *The Antinomies of Postmodernity*   *1*

PART TWO   *Utopia, Modernism, and Death*   *73*

PART THREE   *The Constraints of Postmodernism*   *129*

Bibliography   *207*

Index   *211*

Photo Credits   *215*

Introduction

The three chapters in this book, which origi-
nally took the form of lectures in the annual
Wellek Library Lecture series at the University
of California at Irvine in 1991, have a somewhat deeper interrelationship, which their new
title seeks to emphasize. Even after the "end
of history," there has seemed to persist some
historical curiosity of a generally systemic—
rather than a merely anecdotal—kind: not
merely to know what will happen next, but as

a more general anxiety about the larger fate or destiny of our system or mode of production as such—about which individual experience (of a postmodern kind) tells us that it must be eternal, while our intelligence suggests this feeling to be most improbable indeed, without coming up with plausible scenarios as to its disintegration or replacement. It seems to be easier for us today to imagine the thoroughgoing deterioration of the earth and of nature than the breakdown of late capitalism; perhaps that is due to some weakness in our imaginations.

I have come to think that the word *postmodern* ought to be reserved for thoughts of this kind. The term and its various substantives seem instead to have evolved into various partisan expressions of value, mostly turning on the affirmation or repudiation of this or that vision of pluralism. But these are arguments better conducted in concrete social terms (those of the various feminisms, or the new social movements, for example). Postmodernism as an ideology, however, is better grasped as a symptom of the deeper structural changes in our society and its culture as a whole—or in other words in the mode of production.

Inasmuch as those changes still remain tendencies, however, and our analyses of actuality are governed by the selection of what we think will persist or develop, any attempt to say what postmodernism is can scarcely be separated from the even more problematic attempt to say where it is going—in short, to disengage its contradictions, to imagine its consequences (and the consequences of those consequences), and to conjecture the shape of its agents and institutions in some more fully developed maturity of what can now at best only be trends and currents. All postmodernism theory is thus a telling of the future, with an imperfect deck. Whether the analysis of the "current situation" has always amounted to this is an interesting question, one that I do not want to decide: perhaps the millenarian visions of modernism were somehow closer to the present of its visionaries than our visions today, about which we are assured that whatever they are they are neither millenarian nor Utopian.

At any rate, each chapter of this book attempts a diagnosis of the cultural present with a view toward opening a perspective onto a future they are clearly incapable of forecasting in any prophetic sense. But they do this on the basis of three relatively distinct methodological operations. The first chapter, on the antinomies of contemporary thought and ideology, ignores the discontinuities of separate opinions and positions and searches out crucial points at which even opposing positions seem to share a common conceptual dilemma, which is nowhere brought to light and reflected on in its own terms. The working fiction here is therefore that a host of specific positions and texts (in themselves more or less coherent and self-contained) share an unrepresentable ground that can only be conveyed as a mass of logical paradoxes and unresolvable conceptual paralogisms. These cannot, of course, be "solved" from any higher perspective, and I imagine that there exist many more of the antinomies than those enumerated here (or at least that they come in many more realizations, which a logician might, to be sure, reduce to some simpler primal form). What it seemed to me useful to do, in an ambitious idea that here remains the merest sketch, is to suggest an outside and an unrepresentable exterior to many of the issues that seem most crucial in contemporary (that is to say, postmodern) debate. The future lies entangled in that unrepresentable outside like so many linked genetic messages. This chapter, then, is an experiment at giving a certain representation to the way in which contradiction works, so that it might be called *dialectical* on one use of that term, even though what it sets out from is a stalled or arrested dialectic.

To the same degree, the final chapter might be characterized in some very general sense as *structural,* since unlike the first chapter it posits a very rigid notion of closure, in the form of Greimas's semiotic rectangle, with the its finite number of conceptual combinations and possibilities. This semiotic technology is now used to prospect and explore, not ideological variety, as in the first chapter, but aesthetic multiplicity and "pluralism." Indeed, it springs from a certain exasperation with myself and with others, who have so frequently expressed their enthusiasm with the boundless and ungovernable richness of modern artistic—in this case architectural—forms and styles, which, freed from the telos of modern, are now "lawless" in any number of novel and invigorating or enabling ways (which one had better not call "new" or original, since it was the very release from that old modernist taboo of Newness that, like a magic wand, freed the postmodern to its unimaginable contemporary flourishing). In my own case it was the conception of "style"—very familiar to me from a previous period—that prevented me for so long from shaking off this impression of illimitable pluralism; but it did so negatively, working through the conviction that personal style as such was no longer possible after the regime of the individual centered subject, while the reduction of an entire period to some generalizable period style such as the baroque or the gothic seemed not merely intolerably idealist but also undialectical; it failed to take account of the role henceforth played in contemporary or postmodern production by the sheer fact of the historicist persistence of all the previous period and world styles well into our own present, which now surcharged those in well-nigh mediatic fashion. The postmodern, in other words, was also constitutively defined by its inclusion of all possible styles and thereby its own incapacity to be globally characterized, from the outside, by any specific style as such: its resistance in other words to aesthetic or stylistic *totalization* (and it is this aesthetic resistance that is probably always meant when polemics are incorrectly waged against political or philosophical totalization).

I then overestimated the variety of actually existing postmodern "styles" and seemed to have forgotten the fundamental

structuralist lesson that a totality is a combination or permutation scheme, endowed with a closure of its own no matter
how ineffably fluid and dynamic its processes may be: which is
to say that any attempt to conceptualize such processes—in
chaos or catastrophe theory, for example—can do so only by
endowing them with a representation that is itself a mode of
closure. But there is a fundamental difference between the
closure of the situation and the closure of the responses to it:
the latter is alone idealistic, since it posits a structural limit in
the response, the act or work or style, rather than in the
material situation itself. I was looking for that limit in the
architectural works themselves (had it been possible to find it,
as it is in certain historical periods, the formal limit would
have taken the form of a specific period style). In reality,
however, the structural limit is to be found in the situation or
dilemma to which the individual architects and their specific
and unique projects all have to respond in some way or
another.

Anyone who thinks my account is somehow offensive and
insulting to the architects themselves, all artists of a rare talent
whom I admire greatly, has not understood that creativity lies
in the response rather than in the initial givens and raw
materials of the situation itself. And the error about freedom
and indeterminacy that forms the philosophical and metaphysical accompaniment to such discussions is of a similar kind: it
attributes some old-fashioned deterministic causality to a mapping of structural limits for which causality must rather be
redefined as the *conditions of possibility*. Like Gide's Lafcadio,
nobody wants to be predictable and fully known in advance
(and they think God, "totalization," or determinism tend to do
that, to have you predestined down to the smallest misguided
effort at sham creativity or the vain exercise of a spurious free
will). The doctrine of limits goes very far indeed, deep into
the individual psyche and its structural formation as a kind of
inner situation within which a reduced kind of individual

freedom is required to operate. It does not dispel or erase agency altogether—rather, it makes the specification of such agency alone possible.

My little chart of the closure of the architectural postmodernisms—itself nothing more than a sketch, as in the first chapter—does not try to forecast the future by projecting it as what will overcome these oppositions (or be neutralized and paralyzed by them). Rather, it is inspired by Hegel's old idea that when we identify a boundary or a limit (Kant's block, in his case), we nonetheless modify that limited situation, that situation or experience of absolute limits, ever so slightly by drawing the situation as a whole inside itself and making the limit now part of what it had hitherto limited, and thereby subject to modification in its own turn. But this vague aim or ambition is then at one with the limits of structuralism as well, whose precisions always began to run off into the blurred and the watery when it came to the moment of truth or decision, and the prospect of a certain praxis.

My remaining chapter, then, the second one, which stands out like a sore thumb from these other, postmodern discussions no less than from the order of my commentary here, is probably best characterized formally in more Freudian or depth-psychological terms, as a matter of repression and negation, even sublimation, and probably of mourning as well. For here we confront what has vanished from the postmodern scene, in every but a literal sense (since it was very precisely during the sway of a tendentially global postmodern culture, in the 1980s, that this fundamental text of Platonov, along with others, was rediscovered and printed for the first time).

Here, then, we have to do with what must now be called Second World culture, an emergent socialist culture whose development, in its Eastern or Slavic form, has been cut short. I would want to argue—at least this second chapter presupposes such an argument—not only that there was a specific Second World culture, whose originality was defined in part by its distance from commodity fetishism, but also that what has in the West been called dissidence was largely part of that as well, as witness Solzhenitsyn's rage at finding that Vermont, noncommunist although it may have been, was as corrupt and Western, as capitalist, as any Slavophile or Soviet communist might have always predicted it would turn out to be. Dissidence is thus a Second World form of intellectual life, and the anticommunist opinions of its aesthetic practitioners no more make them over into First World writers and artists than the opposition to the State over here makes us nonbourgeois.

I say this because, although in my view Platonov's Utopia is nonironic, the grisly pictures and visions it yields might well be taken as ironic by readers unforewarned, and might be supposed to be arguments against communism rather than expressions of the experience of it. I want to argue, in other words, that the very violence of *Chevengur,* for some of us almost intolerable, is the very price to be paid for the authenticity of its Utopian impulse (as that produces its text in waves of new, ever self-canceling figuration): the price for what rescues Utopia from the edulcoration of its status in the West. But it is all of this that must be worked through in detail—all the raw dust and savagery of the Utopian vision and the half-baked simple-mindedness of its village citizens—in order for us to grasp once more what is omitted from the postmodern worldview, or better still, what had to have been repressed from it with some new violence in its own right, for that "worldview" (which is of course not really a worldview in the older sense but rather a positivist and technocratic cancellation of all of those) to come into being in the first place. This chapter, then, serves as something of a slow movement for the others, and sets in place some echoes of a past whose structural absence must also presumably define our future to come almost better than some of the most obvious components of our present.

The inscription of the name of an old friend, in thanks for his intellectual and social hospitality, will also define these pages with yet another kind of limit, and juxtapose a global (but still Western) postmodernity with the immense heterotopia of China itself.

Killingworth, Connecticut

THE SEEDS OF TIME

The Antinomies of Postmodernity

It is conventional to distinguish an antinomy from a contradiction, not least because folk wisdom implies that the latter is susceptible of a solution or a resolution, whereas the former is not. In that sense, the antinomy is a cleaner form of language than the contradiction. With it, you know where you stand; it states two propositions that are radically, indeed absolutely, incompatible, take it or leave it. Whereas the contradiction is a matter of partialities and aspects; only some of it is incompatible with the accompanying proposition; indeed, it may have more to do with forces, or the state of things, than with words or logical implications. Contradictions are supposed, in the long run, to be productive; whereas antinomies—take Kant's classic one: the world has a beginning, the world has no beginning—offer nothing in the way of a handle, no matter how diligently you turn them around and around.

All of which probably implies that the contradiction is a singular substance, about which several different, seemingly contradictory, things get said; a little sweat and ingenuity then suffices to show that the two contradictory things are somehow related, or the same—the one implied by the other, or following from it in some unsuspected way. In that case, it is the situation that accounts for the disparity, in its very incompleteness generating the multiple perspectives that make us think the matter at hand is now *x,* or *y;* or better still, *x*-like and *y*-like all at the same time. Whereas the antinomy is clearly and unequivocally two separate things: *y* or *x;* and that in such a way that the question of a situation or a context fades away altogether.

The age is clearly enough more propitious for the antinomy than the contradiction. Even in Marxism itself, the latter's spiritual homeland, the most advanced tendencies have nagged and worried at the contradiction, as at some last inexpungeable remnant of idealism capable of reinfecting the system in some fatally old-fashioned way (like vapors or brain fever). Thus the most brilliant of all Marx's commentators, Lucio Coletti, began to play Kant off against the dialectic, and to persuade himself (and us) that contradictions were not in nature, since there all phenomena are positive. I think he was wrong about this, as far as Kant was concerned, since in Kant it is precisely only "in nature" (or rather, in what he calls the "real in appearance") that oppositions do exist; in fact, the critical position with which Coletti began to flirt here is called positivism, and it led him out of Marxism altogether. (There can be no doubt, however, that the return to Kant, today, has generally had the value of an antidialectical move.)

A still greater and more influential Marxian theorist, Louis Althusser, seems to have conceived of his mission as a resolutely modernizing (or postmodernizing) one; as the intent to cleanse Marxism of all its Hegelian—which is to say Germanic and idealist—baggage. He went so far as to cast doubt on the concept of mediation (which might, indeed, in a pinch be substituted by that of transcoding), but one has it on good evidence that he meant to forge ahead and ultimately to stigmatize and exorcize the very notion of contradiction itself: something he in fact inspired his more distant anti-Marxist followers Hindess and Hirst to go on and do. Their example makes one wonder whether any other way of doing it could have left Marxism as such intact either.

If these were the most advanced trends at work within Marxism, what was going on outside it need perhaps not be imagined. Equivalents of the general notion of contradiction persisted in the various psychoanalyses; structuralism itself—even while Lévi-Strauss continued to emphasize the importance for him of both the Marxist and the Freudian conceptions of contradiction—tended rather, along with emergent semiotics, to reinforce the slippage of the category of contradiction toward the more logical one of the antinomy. But the currency of this second term (itself equally of no interest to the prevailing forms of positivism) we seem to owe primarily to deconstruction, where it became, particularly in the hands of Paul de Man, an instrument for showing up everything that was self-conflicted about a thought and its language at the same time that its essential paralysis and nonproductivity was foregrounded in a kind of conceptual freeze-frame. Something of a return toward the contradiction, however, seems on the agenda today, in Hegelian Lacanianism, where Slavoj Žižek's notion of the "symptom" proposes a rethinking of both Freud and Marx.

My own feeling has been that, rather than positing a situation in which we have to choose between these two categories (contradiction standing for the modernist option perhaps, while antinomy offers a more postmodern one), it might be worthwhile using them both concurrently and against one other, insofar as each is uniquely equipped to problematize the other in its most vital implications. The pair do not themselves form an opposition, exactly (although it would be an amusing logical exercise to pretend they do, and to try to decide whether their difference amounts to an antinomy or is itself merely one more contradiction); rather, they stand as each other's bad conscience, and as a breath of suspicion that clings to the concept itself. To wonder whether an antinomy is not really a contradiction in disguise; to harbor the nagging thought that what we took to be a contradiction was really little more than an antinomy—these pointed reciprocal doubts can do the mind no harm and may even do it some good.

That being said, I will organize my symptomatology accordingly, and operate as though an antinomy were a *symptom* of a contradiction: this may presuppose a multidimensional model or image, as well as the notion that our own age—that of technocratic positivism and experiential nominalism—is one- or two-dimensional by choice just as much as by historical development. So it is that depth forms (if any exist, like prehistoric monsters) tend to be projected up upon the surface in the anamorphic flatness of a scarcely recognizable afterimage, lighting up on the board in the form of a logical paradox or a textual paralogism. We have to swim in both these worlds at once; learn to work the remote-control glove within the contamination chamber; posit a noumenal shadow world of seismographic movements and shoulderings that inscribes itself with grotesque delicacy as minute and pencil-thin lines on the graph.

These figures suggest that the deeper problem with the concept of contradiction—a problem that cannot be resolved and that has no equivalent in anything surrounding the concept of the antinomy—is representational. Contradiction is always one step before representation: if you show it in its conflicted moment, you freeze it over so rigidly that it tends to take on the form of the antinomy. If on the contrary you anticipate its resolution, you empty it of all its negativity and generate the impression of a rigged ballot, a put-up job, a sham conflict whose outcome has already carefully been arranged in advance. Or, if you prefer, the sheer fact of having each foot in a different irreconcilable world—Antigone versus Creon— means that a representation that wants to remain true to those distinct worlds and their laws can only show its credentials and document its authenticity by failing to provide some third representational language in which they both seem falsely reconciled. This situation means, however, that the philosophical languages in which contradiction is accounted for will always be deficient and arouse a properly philosophical dissatisfaction: even Hegel's grand architectonic stages tend to fall on one side or another of the central tension, and seem to intensify into pictures of a dramatic or historical, essentially narrative scene on the one hand, or else to thin out into those formal abstractions of identity and difference that are finally the domain of the antinomy rather than of the contradiction itself.

Such tendencies are everywhere in contemporary thought, and they can be explained as the results and consequences of the latter's fundamental trends, which I have characterized as positivism and nominalism (leaving aside the interesting matter of the relationship between these two things, which can be thought of as objective and subjective respectively, as the realms of the system and of the subject). This "explanation" is, of course, one always wants to hasten to add, in current language, only one of the narratives we can tell about the current situation. But it is a good story, which can be foreshadowed by way of Adolf Loos's notorious attack on ornament in architecture and design, in which such figuration was assimilated to crime and the antisocial on the one hand, and degeneracy (still a popular concept in that period) on the other. After positivism and pragmatism, indeed, abstraction itself comes to be thought of as something like ornament: superfluous and unpractical, self-indulgent, "speculative" and metaphysical, the signs and indices of a slovenly and sinful leisure and privilege. Getting rid of the old names, of all those abstractions that still reek of universalism or generality, cleaving with even greater determination to the empirical and the actual, stigmatizing the residual as philosophical in the bad sense, which is to say as sheer idealism, without thereby lapsing into a materialism equally occult and metaphysical—these are the postmodern watchwords, which were once a guide to a kind of Wittgensteinian witch-hunt in the name of the health and purity of the language, but now circulate through the economy as effortlessly as the deliveries at your corner supermarket.

It is a reduction that can presumably not succeed; but its current hegemony not only means that much of what characterized classical philosophy must disappear but also that there can remain very little, in the way of the syncategoremic abstraction, to bind together the disparate words and syllables of a nominalistic and fragmented set of perceptions. This is the situation and the crisis from which two large and crude sorting systems tend to reemerge, from archaic time, like the return of the repressed. They are the grandest and most empty of all abstractions whose earliest (Western) avatar can be witnessed in formation in the primal indistinctions of the first forms of secular thought in the pre-Socratics: the categories of Identity and Difference (which Kant and Hegel knew as concepts or categories of *reflexion*), the most formal of all, which now survive to constitute the last extant evolutionary conceptual species, insofar as they have the advantage of seeming to offer virtually no content in their own right, no smuggled philosophical contraband, as neutral and value-free as technology or the market.

These are nondialectical categories, and you would have to bend them out of shape with some violence to appropriate them for Hegel's "identity of identity and non-identity." Identity and Difference are, rather, the realm and the domain of the antinomy as such: something they readily offer to demonstrate by effortlessly turning into one another at the slightest pretext. Rather than as dialectical, even as an arrested or paralyzed dialectic, it might be better to characterize them in terms of a kind of reversal of Freud's (modernist) conception of the "antithetical sense of primal words," which drew our attention to the way in which, etymologically X-rayed, a single term proved to carry within itself, along with its primordial meaning, the latter's negation or opposite (most famously, *heimlich,* what is most familiar and homely, also turns out to mean the same thing as *unheimlich,* what is most uncanny, weird and strange). Here, on the contrary, as for example in that specific postmodern antinomy whereby what is anti-Utopian turns out to be Utopian in its most fundamental significance, it is (as we shall see) the antitheses that turn out to be, somehow, "the same." Paradoxes of this kind are not, however, in postmodern discourse, the telltale scandals or anomalies (the failure of a star to correspond infinitestimally to its predicted trajectory) that used to incite to the rethinking of the paradigm as a whole. Here, rather, they provide the bread-and-butter concepts of all of so-called contemporary theory (or theoretical discourse), and offer training in state-of-the-art mental gymnastics not unrelated to the verbal games and logical tricks rehearsed by the sophists (as Lyotard has pointed out).

In what follows, however, we will collect a few of these

paradoxes for examination as symptoms rather than as occasions for demonstrating something about the structural incapacity of the mind itself, or of its languages. This will take the form of brief evocations of four distinct postmodern antinomies, about which one is of course free to wonder whether they are not all fundamentally the same thing, a possibility to which we will return in the conclusion to this chapter. The first two antinomies concern Kant's "a priori representations," namely time and space, which we have generally come to think of in historical terms as implicit formal frames that nonetheless vary according to the mode of production. We may presumably, then, learn something about our own mode of production from the ways in which we tend to think of change and permanence, or variety and homogeneity—ways that prove to have as much to do with space as with time.

The second pair of antinomies would seem to have more to do with the spatial ways in which we fantasize the possibility of the transformation of our system as a whole. The third antinomy, indeed, raises the issue of naturalism in the strict sense, of nature and human nature, or of the absence of such limits and constraints; while the final one, as I promised, takes up the matter of Utopia (as a goal of all change) and of its many contemporary critics and enemies who try today even more enthusiastically than in earlier periods to persuade us to agree that this is indeed the best of all possible worlds.

I

But time is today a function of speed, and evidently perceptible only in terms of its rate, or velocity as such: as though the old Bergsonian opposition between measurement and life, clock time and lived time, had dropped out, along with that virtual eternity or slow permanence without which Valéry thought the very idea of a work as such was likely to die out (something he seems to have been confirmed in thinking).

What emerges then is some conception of change without its opposite: and to say so is then helplessly to witness our first two antinomies folding back into each other, since from the vantage point of change it becomes impossible to distinguish space from time, or object from subject. The eclipse of inner time (and its organ, the "intimate" time sense) means that we read our subjectivity off the things outside: Proust's old hotel rooms, like old retainers, respectfully reminded him every morning how old he was, and whether he was on vacation or "at home," and where—that is to say, they told him his name and issued him an identity, like a visiting card on a silver salver. As for habit, memory, recognition, material things do that for us (the way the servants were supposed to do our living, according to Villiers de l'Isle Adam). Subjectivity is an objective matter, and it is enough to change the scenery and the setting, refurnish the rooms, or destroy them in an aerial bombardment for a new subject, a new identity, miraculously to appear on the ruins of the old.

The end of the subject-object dualism, however—for which so many ideologues have yearned for so long—carries with it hidden retroparadoxes, like concealed explosives: Virilio's, for example, which shows how the seeming speed of the outside world is itself a function of the demands of representation. Not, perhaps, the result of some new subjective idea of velocity that projects itself onto an inert exterior, as in stereotypes of classical idealism, but rather technology versus nature. The apparatus—and very specifically the photographic and filmic one—makes its own demands on reality, which, as in the Gulf War, reality then scrambles to fulfill (like a time-lapse photo in which the photographer himself can be seen breathlessly sliding into place at the end of the row of already posing faces): "[T]he disappearance of the proximity effect in the prosthesis of accelerated travel made it necessary to create a wholly simulated appearance that would restore three-dimensionality to the message in full. Now a holographic prosthesis of the military commander's inertia was to be communicated to the viewer, extending his look in time and space by means of constant flashes, here and there, today and yesterday . . . Already evident in the flashback and then in feedback, this miniaturization of chronological meaning was the direct result of a military technology in which events always unfolded in theoretical time" (Virilio, 59–60).

Such a "return of the repressed" (an old-fashioned, now relatively metaphorical name for it to be sure) means that eliminating the subject does not leave us with the object *wie es eigentlich gewesen,* but rather with a multiplicity of simulacra. Virilio's point, like that of so many others today, is that it is the cinema that is the truly decentered subject, perhaps indeed the only one: the Deleuzian schizo being only a confused and contradictory idea alongside this apparatus that absorbs the former subject-object pole triumphantly into itself. But it raises the embarrassing secondary question of whether, in that case, there ever was a (centered) subject to begin with: did we ever have to wait? Is boredom a figment of the imagination along with its cousin eternity? Was there a time when things did not seem to change? What did we do before machines? All flesh is grass: and life in the ancient *polis* strikes us as being more fragile and ephemeral than anything in the modern city, even though we ought to be able to remember how many changes this last has undergone. It is as though an illusion of slower permanence accompanies the lived present like an optical projection, masking a change that only becomes visible when it falls outside the temporal frame.

But to put it this way is to measure a gap and to assure ourselves of everything that is radically different from the modernist form-projects and the modernist "time-senses" in the postmodern dispensation, where the formerly classical has itself been unmasked as sheer fashion, albeit the fashion of a slower, vaster world that took ages to cross by caravan or caravel, and through whose thickened time, as through a viscous element, items descended so slowly as to acquire a patina that seemed to transform their contingencies into the necessities of a meaningful tradition. For a world population, the languages of Periclean Athens can no longer be any more normative than that of other tribal styles (although it is very easy to imagine a cultural United Nations Security Council operation in which the "great civilizations" pooled their various classical traditions with a view toward imposing some more generally "human" classical canon): time thereby also becomes multicultural, and the hitherto airtight realms of demography and of industrial momentum begin to seep into each other, as though there were some analogies between great crowds of people and dizzying rates of speed. Both then spell the end of the modern in some renewed and paradoxical conjunction, as when the new styles seem exhausted by virtue of their very proliferation, while their bearers, the individual creators, prophets, geniuses, and seers, suddenly find themselves unwanted owing to sheer population density (if not the realization of the democratic ethos as such).

That the new absolute temporality has everything to do with the urban my references have suggested, without underscoring the requirement in that case of revising traditional notions of the urban as such, in order to accommodate its postnaturality to technologies of communication as well as of production and to mark the decentered, well-nigh global, scale on which what used to be the city is deployed. The modern still had something to do with the arrogance of city people over against the provincials, whether this was a provinciality of peasants, other and colonized cultures, or simply the precapitalist past itself: that deeper satisfaction of being *"absolument moderne"* is dissipated when modern technologies are everywhere, there are no longer any provinces, and even the past comes to seem like an alternate world, rather than an imperfect, privative stage of this one. Meanwhile, those "modern" city dwellers or metropolitans of earlier decades themselves came from the country or at least could still register the coexistence of uneven worlds; they could measure change in ways that become impossible once modernization is even relatively completed (and no longer some isolated, unnatural, and unnerving process that stands out to the naked eye). It is an unevenness and a coexistence that can also be registered in a sense of loss, as with the slow partial changes and demolitions of Baudelaire's Paris, which almost literally serve as the objective correlative of his experience of passing time: in Proust all this, although apparently more intensely elegiac (and in any case surcharging the text of Baudelaire itself), has already been subjectivized, as though it were the self and its past that were regretted and not its houses (but Proust's language knows better: *"la muraille de l'escalier, où je vis monter le reflet de sa bougie, n'existe plus depuis longtemps"* [I, 36], as does his spatial plot construction). Today the very meaning of demolition as such has been modified, along with that of building: it has become a generalized postnatural process that calls into question the very concept of change itself and the inherited notion of time that accompanied it.

These paradoxes are perhaps easier to dramatize in the philosophical and critical realm, than in the aesthetic one, let alone in urbanism as such. For demolition has surely defined the modern intellectual's vocation ever since the ancien régime tended to identify its mission with critique and opposition to established institutions and ideas: what better figure to characterize the strong form of the cultural intellectual from the Enlightenment *philosophes* all the way to Sartre (who has been called the last of the classical intellectuals), if not beyond? It is a figure that has seemed to presuppose an omnipresence of Error, variously defined as superstition, mystification, ignorance, class ideology, and philosophical idealism (or "metaphysics"), in such a way that to remove it by way of the operations of demystification leaves a space in which therapeutic anxiety goes hand in hand with heightened self-consciousness and reflexivity in a variety of senses, if not, indeed, with Truth as such. By attempting to restore, alongside this negative tradition, the intellectual's older mission of the restoration of meaning, Ricoeur sharply dramatized everything the various strands of what he called "the hermeneutics of suspicion" had in common, from the Enlightenment and its relationship to religion all the way to the deconstructive relation to "Western metaphysics," emphasizing above all the three great formative moments of Marx, Nietzsche, and Freud, to which even post-modern intellectuals still owe joint allegiance in one form or another.

What has changed is then perhaps the character of the terrain in which these operations are carried out: just as the transitional period between aristocratic and clerical, ancien-régime societies and mass-democratic industrial capitalist ones has been must longer and slower than we tend to believe (Arno Mayer suggests that significant remnants of the former survived in Europe until the end of World War II), so also the objective role of intellectuals to implement modernization's cultural revolution long remained a progressive one. But the process itself has often tended to impress observers and partici-pants alike by its self-perpetuating and indeed self-devouring energies. It is not only the Revolution that eats its own children; any number of visions of pure negativity as such, from Hegel's account of freedom and the Terror to the Frank-furt School's grim theory of the "dialectic of enlightenment" as an infernal machine, bent on extirpating all traces of transcen-dence (including critique and negativity itself).

Such visions seem even more relevant for one-dimensional societies like our own, from which the residual, in the forms of habits and practices of older modes of production, has been tendentially eliminated, so that it might be possible to hypothesize a modification or displacement in the very func-tion of ideology-critique itself. This is at least the position of Manfredo Tafuri, who offers a kind of functionalist analysis of the avant-garde intellectual, whose "anti-institutional phase" essentially involved "the criticism of outworn values" (70). The very success of such a mission, however, coterminous with the modernizing struggles of capital itself, "serves to prepare a clean-swept platform from which to depart in discovery of the new 'historic tasks' of intellectual work" (70). Not surprisingly, Tafuri identifies these new "modernizing" tasks with rationalization as such: "what the ideologies of the avant-garde introduced as a proposal for social behavior was the transformation of traditional ideology into Utopia, as a prefiguration of an abstract final moment of development coincident with a global rationalization, with a positive realization of the dialectic" (62); Tafuri's formulations become less cryptic when one understands that for him Keynesianism is to be understood as a planification, a rationalization, of the future as such.

Thus seen, demystification in the contemporary period has its own secret "ruse of history," its own inner function and concealed world-historical mission; namely, by destroying traditional societies (not merely the Church and the old aristocracies but above all the peasants and their modes of agricultural production, their common lands, and their villages), to sweep the globe clean for the manipulations of the great corporations: to prepare a purely *fungible* present in which space and psyches alike can be processed and remade at will, with a "flexibility" with which the creativity of the ideologues busy coining glowing new adjectives to describe the potentialities of "post-Fordism" can scarcely keep up. Demolition, under these circumstances, begins to take on new and ominously urbanistic overtones, and to connote the speculations of the developers far more than the older heroic struggles of oppositional intellectuals; while just such objections to and critiques of demolition itself are relegated to a tiresome moralizing and undermine themselves by virtue of their vivid dramatization of outmoded mentalities that are better off being demolished anyhow (*"denn alles, was entsteht, / Ist wert, dass es zugrunde geht"*).

These are now media paradoxes, which result from the speed and tempo of the critical process, as well as the way in which all ideological and philosophical positions as such have in the media universe been transformed into their own "representations" (as Kant might put it)—in other words into images of themselves and caricatures in which identifiable slogans substitute for traditional beliefs (the beliefs having indeed been forced to transform themselves into just such recognizable ideological positions in order to operate in the media marketplace). This is the situation in which it is easier to grasp the progressive value of conservative or residual modes of resistance to the new thing than to evaluate the range of ostensibly left-liberal positions (which, as in Tafuri's model, often functionally prove to be indistinguishable from the structural requirements of the system itself). The diagnosis also projects the mirage of some possible sound barrier, like a telltale line blurring away against the sky; and indeed the obvious question of how much speed the human organism can bear may play its part in the naturalist revivals that will be mentioned later on, in the third section of this chapter; while the new fact itself does seem to offer a fleeting but vivid dramatization of Engels's old law about the transformation of quantity into quality (or at least of that "law" 's afterimage).

In this form, the paradox from which we must set forth is the equivalence between an unparalleled rate of change on all the levels of social life and an unparalleled standardization of everything—feelings along with consumer goods, language along with built space—that would seem incompatible with just such mutability. It is a paradox that can still be conceptualized, but in inverse ratios: that of modularity, for example, where intensified change is enabled by standardization itself, where prefabricated modules, everywhere from the media to a henceforth standardized private life, from commodified

nature to uniformity of equipment, allow miraculous rebuild-
ings to succeed each other at will, as in fractal video. The
module would then constitute the new form of the object (the
new result of reification) in an informational universe: that
Kantian point in which raw material is suddenly organized by
categories into an appropriate unit.

But the paradox can also incite us to rethink our conception
of change itself. If absolute change in our society is best
represented by the rapid turnover in storefronts, prompting
the philosophical question as to what has really changed when
video stores are replaced by T-shirt shops, then Barthes's
structural formulation comes to have much to recommend it,
namely, that it is crucial to distinguish between rhythms of
change inherent to the system and programmed by it, and a
change that replaces one entire system by another one altogether. But that is a point of view that revives paradoxes of
Zeno's sort, which derive from the Parmenidean conception
of Being itself, which, as it *is* by definition, cannot be thought
of as even momentarily becoming, let alone failing to be for
the slightest instant.

The "solution" to this particular paradox lies of course in
the realization (strongly insisted on by Althusser and his disci-
ples) that each system—better still, each "mode of production"—produces a temporality that is specific to it: it is only if
we adopt a Kantian and ahistorical view of time as some
absolute and empty category that the peculiarly repetitive
temporality of our own system can become an object of
puzzlement and lead to the reformulation of these old logical
and ontological paradoxes.

Yet it may not be without its therapeutic effects to continue
for one long moment to be mesmerized by the vision attributed to Parmenides, which however little it holds for nature
might well be thought to capture a certain truth of our social
and historical moment: a gleaming science-fictional stasis in
which appearances (simulacra) arise and decay ceaselessly,

without the momentous stasis of everything that is flickering for the briefest of instants or even momentarily wavering in its ontological prestige.

Here, it is as if the logic of fashion had, accompanying the multifarious penetration of its omnipresent images, begun to bind and identify itself with the social and psychic fabric in some ultimately inextricable way, which tends to make it over into the very logic of our system as a whole. The experience and the value of perpetual change thereby comes to govern language and feelings, fully as much as the buildings and the garments of this particular society, to the point at which even the relative meaning allowed by uneven development (or "nonsynchronous synchronicity") is no longer comprehensible, and the supreme value of the New and of innovation, as both modernism and modernization grasped it, fades away against a steady stream of momentum and variation that at some outer limit seems stable and motionless.

What then dawns is the realization that no society has ever been so standardized as this one, and that the stream of human, social, and historical temporality has never flowed quite so homogeneously. Even the great boredom or ennui of classical modernism required some vantage point or fantasy subject position outside the system; yet our seasons are of the post-natural and postastronomical television or media variety, triumphantly artificial by way of the power of their National Geographic or Weather Channel images: so that their great rotations—in sports, new model cars, fashion, television, the school year or *rentrée,* etc.—simulate formerly natural rhythms for commercial convenience and reinvent such archaic categories as the week, the month, the year imperceptibly, without any of the freshness and violence of, say, the innovations of the French revolutionary calendar.

What we now begin to feel, therefore—and what begins to emerge as some deeper and more fundamental constitution of postmodernity itself, at least in its temporal dimension—is that henceforth, where everything now submits to the perpetual change of fashion and media image, nothing can change any longer. This is the sense of the revival of that "end of History" Alexandre Kojève thought he could find in Hegel and Marx, and which he took to mean some ultimate achievement of democratic equality (and the value equivalence of individual economic and juridical subjects) in both American capitalism and Soviet communism, only later identifying a significant variant of it in what he called Japanese *"snobisme,"* but that we can today identify as postmodernity itself (the free play of masks and roles without content or substance). In another sense, of course, this is simply the old "end of ideology" with a vengeance, and cynically plays on the waning of collective hope in a particularly conservative market climate. But the end of History is also the final form of the temporal paradoxes we have tried to dramatize here: namely that a rhetoric of absolute change (or "permanent revolution" in some trendy and meretricious new sense) is, for the postmodern, no more satisfactory (but not less so) than the language of absolute identity and unchanging standardization cooked up by the great corporations, whose concept of innovation is best illustrated by the neologism and the logo and their equivalents in the realm of built space, "lifestyle," corporate culture, and psychic programming. The persistence of the Same through absolute Difference—the same street with different buildings, the same culture through momentous new sheddings of skin—discredits change, since henceforth the only conceivable radical change would consist in putting an end to change itself. But here the antinomy really does result in the blocking or paralysis of thought, since the impossibility of thinking another system except by way of the cancellation of this one ends up discrediting the Utopian imagination itself, which is fantasized, as we shall see later, as the loss of everything we know experientially, from our libidinal investments to our psychic habits, and in particular the artificial excitements of consumption and fashion.

Parmenidean stasis or Being to be sure knows at least one irrevocable event, namely death and the passage of the generations: insofar as the system of Parmenidean simulacrum or illusion is a very recent one, constituted in what we call postmodernity, the temporality of the generations in all their mortal discontinuity is not yet visible in results, except retroactively and as a materialist historiographic imperative. But death itself, as the very violence of absolute change, in the form of the nonimage—not even bodies rotting off stage but rather something persistent like an odor that circulates through the luminous immobility of this world without time—is inescapable and meaningless, since any historical framework that would serve to interpret and position individual deaths (at least for their survivors) has been destroyed. A kind of absolute violence then, the abstraction of violent death, is something like the dialectical correlative to this world without time or history.

But it is more appropriate to conclude this section with a remark about the relationship of this temporal paradox— absolute change equals stasis—to the dynamics of the new global system itself, for here too we can observe an effacement of the temporalities that seemed to govern an older period of modernity, of modernism and modernization alike. For in that older period, most Third World societies were torn by a penetration of Western modernization that generated over against itself—in all the variety of cultural forms characteristic of those very different societies—a counterposition that could generally be described as traditionalism: the affirmation of a cultural (and sometimes religious) originality that had the power to resist assimilation by Western modernity and was indeed preferable to it. Such traditionalism was of course a construction in its own right, brought into being as it were, by the very activities of the modernizers themselves (in some more limited and specific sense than the one now, widely accepted, that all traditions and historical pasts are themselves necessarily invented and constructed). At any rate, what one wants to affirm today is that this second reactive or antimodern term of tradition and traditionalism has everywhere vanished from the reality of the former Third World or colonized societies; where a neotraditionalism (as in certain recent Chinese revivals of Confucianism, or in religious fundamentalisms) is now rather perceived as a deliberate political and collective choice, in a situation in which little remains of a past that must be completely reinvented.

This is to say that, on the one hand, nothing but the modern henceforth exists in Third World societies; but it is also to correct this statement, on the other, with the qualification that under such circumstances, where only the modern exists, "modern" must now be rebaptised postmodern (since what we call modern is the consequence of incomplete modernization and must necessarily define itself against a nonmodern residuality that no longer obtains in postmodernity as such—or rather, whose absence defines this last). Here too then, but on a social and historical level, the temporality that modernization promised (in its various capitalist and communist, productivist forms) has been eclipsed to the benefit of a new condition in which that older temporality no longer exists, leaving an appearance of random changes that are mere stasis, a disorder after the end of history. Meanwhile, it is as though what used to be characterized as the Third World has entered the interstices of the First one, as the latter also demodernizes and deindustrializes, lending the former colonial otherness something of the centered identity of the former metropolis.

With this extension of the temporal paradox on a global scale something else becomes clear as well, a kind of second paradox or antinomy that begins to make its presence felt behind and perhaps even within the first. Indeed, the repeated spatial characterizations of temporality here—from Proust to storefronts, from urban change to global "development"—now begin to remind us that if it is so that postmodernity is characterized by some essential spatialization, then everything we have here been trying to work out in terms of temporality will necessarily have passed through a spatial matrix to come to expression in the first place. If time has in effect been reduced to the most punctual violence and minimal irrevocable change of an abstract death, then we can perhaps affirm that in the postmodern time has become space anyhow. The foundational antinomy of postmodern description lies then in the fact that this former binary opposition, along with identity and difference themselves, no longer is an opposition as such, and ceaselessly reveals itself to have been at one with its other pole in a rather different way than the old dialectical projection back and forth, the classic dialectical metamorphosis. In order to see what this involves, we now necessarily turn to the other spatial antinomy, which apparently we have been rehearsing all along it its temporal version, with a view toward determining whether spatiality has any genuine thematic priority.

2

It is at least certain that the form by which one dimension of the antithesis necessarily expresses itself by way of the figurality of the other, time being required to express itself in spatial terms, is not repeated here; nor is the time-space antithesis symmetrical or reversible in this sense. Space does not seem to require a temporal expression; if it is not what absolutely does without such temporal figurality, then at the very least it might be said that space is what represses temporality and temporal figurality absolutely, to the benefit of other figures and codes. If Difference and Identity are at stake in both the temporal and the spatial antinomy, then the difference preeminent in considerations of space is not so much that of change in any temporal understanding of the form, as rather variety and infinity, metonymy, and—to reach some more influential and seemingly definitive and all-encompassing version—heterogeneity.

Historically, the adventures of homogeneous and heterogeneous space have most often been told in terms of the quotient of the sacred and of the folds in which it is unevenly invested: as for its alleged opposite number, the profane, however, one supposes that it is a projection backward in time of postsacred and commercial peoples to imagine that it was itself any single thing or quality (a nonquality, rather); a projection indeed to think that anything like a simple dualism of the profane and the sacred ever existed as such in the first place. For the sacred can be supposed to have meant heterogeneity and multiplicity in the first place: a nonvalue, an excess, something irreducible to system or to thought, to identity, to the degree to which it not merely explodes itself, but its opposite number, positing the spaces for normal village living alongside the chthonic garbage heaps of the *im-monde* (Lefebvre) but also the empty spaces of waste and desert, the sterile voids that punctuate so many naturally expressive landscapes. For by definition there must also have been as many types or kinds of the sacred as there were powers, and one must drain these words of their feeble archaic overtones before we realize that abstractions such as *sacred* or *power* have, in the face of the realities they were meant to designate, about the same expressive force as the abstraction *color* for the variety of intensities that absorb our gaze.

This also bears on the meaning of landscape, whose secular and painted modern version is a very recent development, as interpreters such as Deleuze or Karatani have so often reminded us. I hesitate to lapse into the fantasies of Romantics like Runge, with his languages of the plants; but they are certainly attractive fantasies, at least until they become socially stabilized in the form of kitsch (with its "language of flowers"). Such notions of a space that is somehow meaningfully organized and on the very point of speech, a kind of articulated thinking that fails to reach its ultimate translation in proposition or concepts, in messages, ultimately find their justification and theoretical defense in Lévi-Strauss's description, in *La Pensée sauvage,* of prephilosophical "perceptual science"; while their aesthetic reaches at least one kind of climax in the anthropologist's classic reading of the Pacific Northwest Coast Indian *Epic of Asdiwal,* where the various landscapes, from frozen inland wastes to the river and the coast itself, speak multiple languages (including those of the economic mode of production itself and of the kinship structure) and emit a remarkable range of articulated messages.

This kind of analysis effectively neutralizes the old opposition between the rational and the irrational (and all the satellite oppositions—primitive versus civilized, male versus female, West versus East—that are grounded on it) by locating the dynamics of meaning in texts that precede conceptual abstraction: a multiplicity of levels is thereby at once opened up that can no longer be assimilated to Weberian rationalization, instrumental thought, the reifications and repressions of the narrowly rational or conceptual. It is thereby to be characterized as heterogeneity; and we can go on to describe the sensory articulations of its object, in the mobile landscapes of *Asdiwal,* as heterogeneous space. As Derrida has famously shown, in one of the inaugural documents of what later comes to be called poststructuralism, Lévi-Strauss's analysis remains somehow centered around homologous meanings: it fails to reach the ultimately aleatory and undecideable; it persists in clinging for dear life to the very concept of meaning proper; and in a situation that ought to put an end to that concept, it does not even attain the openness of Bakhtinian polyphony or heteroglossia, since there is still a collective agency—the tribe—that speaks through its multiplicities.

But that then becomes the failure of Lévi-Strauss to reach true heterogeneity rather than the historical insufficiency of this latter concept as such, about which Bataille's whole life's work demonstrates that it exists in situation and is, like the surrealism from which it derived and that it repudiates, a strategic reaction against a modern state of things. This leads one to wonder whether heterogeneity can in fact mean anything suitably subversive until homogeneity has historically emerged, to confer upon it the value and the force of a specific oppositional tactic. What has to be described, therefore, is not so much the prestige of such forms of multiplicity and excess that overspill the rational modern mind and rebuke it, as rather their values as reactions against it whose projection into the past is at best a doubtful and suspicious matter. The prior object of description is rather the gradual colonization of the world by precisely that homogeneity that it was Bataille's historical mission (as of so many others) to challenge: its tendential conquests, the setting in place of forms of identity that only after the fact allow the anachronistic illusion of heterogeneity and difference to come to seem the logic of what they organized and flattened out.

That process, as far as space is concerned, can surely be identified with some precision: it is the moment in which a Western system of private property in real estate displaces the various systems of land tenure it confronts in the course of its successive enlargements (or, in the European situation itself, from which it gradually emerges for the first time in its own right). Nor does a language of violence—otherwise perfectly appropriate for these supercessions and still observable in course in settler colonies such as Israel and also in the various "transitions to capitalism" in Eastern Europe—convey the way in which the substitution of one legal system for another, more customary one is a matter of calculation and elaborate political strategy (see Guha). The violence was no doubt always implicit in the very conception of ownership as such when applied to the land; it is a peculiarly ambivalent mystery that mortal beings, generations of dying organisms, should have imagined they could somehow *own* parts of the earth in the first place. The older forms of land tenure (as well as the more recent socialist forms, equally varied from country to country) at least posited the collectivity as the immortal governor into whose stewardship portions of the soil are given over; nor has it ever been a simple or easy matter to undo these social relationships and replace them with the apparently more obvious and manageable ones based on individualized ownership and a juridical system of equivalent subjects—East Germany in this respect today rather resembles what the American North had to do to the conquered South after the Civil War; while the Israeli settlements often remind one of the brutal displacement of Native American societies in the West of the United States.

The point is, however, that where the thematic opposition of heterogeneity and homogeneity is invoked, it can only be this brutal process that is the ultimate referent: the effects that result from the power of commerce and then capitalism proper—which is to say, sheer number as such, number now shorn and divested of its own magical heterogeneities and reduced to equivalencies—to seize upon a landscape and flatten it out, reorganize it into a grid of identical parcels, and expose it to the dynamic of a market that now reorganizes space in terms of an identical value. The development of capitalism then distributes that value most unevenly indeed, until at length, in its postmodern moment, sheer speculation, as something like the triumph of spirit over matter, the liberation of the form of value from any of its former concrete or earthly content, now reigns supreme and devastates the very cities and countrysides it created in the process of its own earlier development. But all such later forms of abstract violence and homogeneity derive from the initial parcelization, which translates the money form and the logic of commodity production for a market back onto space itself.

Our own period also teaches us that the fundamental contradiction in this reorganization of space, which seeks to stamp out older and customary forms of collective land tenure (that then swim back into the modern historical imagination in the form of religious or anthropological conceptions of "the sacred" or of archaic heterogeneity), is to be identified as what we equally used to call agriculture itself, when that was associated with a peasantry or even yeoman farmers. In a postmodern global system, in which the tendency of a hitherto overwhelming peasant population to drop to some 7 or 8 percent of the nation can be observed everywhere in the modernizing fully as much as in the "advanced" countries, the relationship between peasant agriculture and traditional culture has become only too clear: the latter follows the former into extinction, and all the great precapitalist cultures prove to have been peasant ones, except where they were based on slavery. (Meanwhile, as for what has until today passed for a capitalist culture—a specifically capitalist "high culture," that is—it can also be identified as the way in which a bourgeoisie imitated and aped the traditions of its aristocratic feudal predecessors, tending also to be eclipsed along with their memory and to give way, along with the older classical bourgeois class consciousness itself, to mass culture—indeed to a specifically American mass culture at that.)

But the very possibility of a new globalization (the expansion of capital beyond its earlier limits in its second, or "imperialist," stage) depended on an agricultural reorganization (sometimes called the green revolution owing to its technological and specifically chemical and biological innovations) that effectively made peasants over into farm workers and great estates or latifundia (as well as village enclaves) over into agribusiness. Pierre-Philippe Rey has indeed suggested that we understand the relationship of modes of production to one another as one of imbrication or articulation, rather than as one of simple supercession: in this respect, he suggests the second or "modern" moment of capital—the stage of imperialism—retained an older precapitalist mode of production in agriculture and kept it intact, exploiting it in tributary fashion, deriving capital by extensive labor, inhuman hours and conditions, from essentially precapitalist relations. The new multinational stage of capital is then characterized by the sweeping away of such enclaves and their utter assimilation into capitalism itself, with its wage labor and working conditions: at this point, agriculture—culturally distinctive and identified in the superstructure as the Other of Nature—now becomes an industry like any other, and the peasants simple workers whose labor is classically commodified in terms of value equivalencies. This is not to say that commodification is evenly distributed over the entire globe or that all areas have been equally modernized or postmodernized; rather, that the tendency toward global commodification is far more visible and imaginable than it was in the modern period, in which tenacious premodern life realities still existed to impede the process. Capital, as Marx showed in the *Grundrisse,* necessarily tends toward the outer limit of a global market that is also its ultimate crisis situation (since no further expansion is then possible): this doctrine is for us today much less abstract than it was in the modern period; it designates a conceptual reality that neither theory nor culture can any longer postpone to some future agenda.

But to say so is to evoke the obliteration of difference on a world scale, and to convey a vision of the irrevocable triumph of spatial homogeneity over whatever heterogeneities might still have been fantasized in terms of global space. I want to stress this as an ideological development, which includes all the ecological fears awakened in our own period (pollution and its accompaniments also standing as a mark of universal commodification and commercialization): for in this situation ideology is not false consciousness but itself a possibility of knowledge, and our constitutive difficulties in imagining a world beyond global standardization are very precisely indices and themselves features of just that standardized reality or being itself.

Such ideological limits, invested with a certain affective terror as a kind of dystopia, are then compensated by other ideological possibilities that come into view when we no longer take the countryside as our vantage point but rather the city and the urban itself. This is of course already an opposition that has left significant traces in the science-fictional or Utopian tradition: the antithesis between a pastoral Utopia and an urban one, and in particular the apparent supercession in the last years of images of a village or tribal Utopia (Ursula Le Guin's *Always Coming Home* of 1985 was virtually the last of those) by visions of an unimaginably dense urban reality (therein nonetheless somehow imagined) that is either explicitly placed on the Utopian agenda, as in Samuel Delany's *Triton* (1976) (or Raymond Williams' prescient forecast that socialism, if it is possible, will not be simpler than all this but far more complicated) or by masquerades under a dystopian appearance whose deeper libidinal excitement, however, is surely profoundly Utopian in spirit (as in most current cyberpunk).

Once again, however, we have to do with the conceptual difficulties in which we are plunged by the disappearance of one of the terms of a formerly functioning binary opposition. The disappearance of Nature—the commodification of the countryside and the capitalization of agriculture itself all over the world—now begins to sap its other term, the formerly urban. Where the world system today tends toward one enormous urban system—tendentially ever more complete modernization promised that, which has however been ratified and delivered in an unexpected way by the communications revolution and its new technologies: a development of which the immediately physical visions, nightmares of the "sprawl" from Boston to Richmond, or the Japanese urban agglomeration, are the merest allegories—the very conception of the city itself and the classically urban loses its significance and no longer seems to offer any precisely delimited objects of study, any specifically differentiated realities. Rather, the urban becomes the social in general, and both of them constitute and lose themselves in a global that is not really their opposite either (as it was in the older dispensation) but something like their outer reach, their prolongation into a new kind of infinity.

Ideologically, what this dissolution of the boundaries of the traditional city and the classically urban enables is a slippage, a displacement, a reinvestment of older urban ideological and libidinal connotations under new conditions. The city always seemed to promise freedom, as in the medieval conception of the urban as the space of escape from the land and from feudal labor and serfdom, from the arbitrary power of the lord: "city air" from this perspective now becomes the very opposite of what Marx famously characterized as "rural idiocy," the narrowness of village manners and customs, the provinciality of the rural, with its fixed ideas and superstitions and its hatred of difference. Here, in contrast to the dreary sameness of the countryside (which is also, however inaccurately, fantasized as a place of sexual repression), the urban classically promised variety and adventure, often linked to crime just as the accompanying visions of pleasure and sexual gratification are inseparable from transgression and illegality.

What happens, then, when even that countryside, even that essentially provincial reality, disappears, becomes standardized, hears the same English, sees the same programs, consumes the same consumer goods, as the former metropolis to which, in the old days, these same provincials and country people longed to go as to a fundamental liberation? I think that the missing second term—provincial boredom, rural idiocy— was preserved, but simply transferred to a different kind of city and a different kind of social reality, namely the Second World city and the social realities of a nonmarket or planned economy. Everyone remembers the overwhelming power of such Cold War iconography, which has perhaps proved even more effective today, after the end of the Cold War and in the thick of the current offensive of market propaganda and rhetoric, than it was in a situation of struggle where visions of terror were more quintessentially operative. Today, however, it is the memory of the imagined drabness of the classic Second World city—with its meager shelves of consumer goods in empty centrals from which the points of light of advertising are absent, streets from which small stores and shops are missing, standardization of clothing fashions (as most emblematically in Maoist China)—that remains ideologically operative in the campaigns for privatization. Jane Jacobs' fundamental identification of a genuine urban fabric and street life with small business is ceaselessly rehearsed ideologically, without any reminder that she thought the diagnosis applied fully as much to the North American or capitalist city in which corporations have equally, but in a different fashion, driven small business out of existence, and created canyons of institutional high-rises without any urban personality at all.

This urban degradation, which characterizes the First World, has, however, been transferred to a separate ideological compartment called postmodernism, where it duly takes its place in the arsenal of attacks on modern architecture and its ideals. As for the Second World city, its vision is rather enlisted in the service of a rather different operation, namely to serve as the visual and experiential *analogon* of a world utterly programmed and directed by human intention, a world therefore from which the contingencies of chance—and thereby the promise of adventure and real life, of libidinal gratification—are also excluded. Conscious intention, the "plan," collective control, are then fantasized as being at one with repression and renunciation, with instinctual impoverishment: and as in the related postmodern polemic, the absence of ornament from the Second World city—as it were the involuntary enactment of Adolf Loos's program—serves as a grim caricature of the puritanical Utopian values of a revolutionary society (just as it had served as that of the equally puritanical Utopian values of high modernism in the other campaign that in certain recent theory in the Eastern countries—in particular Groys' *Gesamtkunstwerk Stalin*—is explicitly linked to this one in an instructive and revealing way).

Only the spatial features of this particular ideological tactic are new: Edmund Burke was of course the first to develop the great antirevolutionary figure, according to which what people consciously and collectively do can only be destructive and a sign of fatal hubris: that only the slow "natural" growth of traditions and institutions can be trusted to form a genuinely human world (a deep suspicion of the will and of unconscious intention that then passes over into a certain Romantic tradition in aesthetics). But Burke's pathbreaking attack on the Jacobins aimed at the middle-class construction and formation of market society itself, about whose commercialism it essentially expressed the fears and anxieties of an older social formation in the process of being superceded. The market people today, however, marshall the same fantasies in defense of a market society now supposed itself to be somehow "natural" and deeply rooted in human nature; they do so against the Promethean efforts of human beings to take collective production into their own hands and, by planning, to control or at least to influence and inflect their own future (something that no longer seems particularly meaningful in a postmodernity in which the very experience of the future as such has come to seem enfeebled, if not deficient).

But this is precisely the ideological and imaginary background against which it is possible to market and to sell the contemporary capitalist city as a well-nigh Bakhtinian carnival of heterogeneities, of differences, libidinal excitement, and a hyperindividuality that effectively decenters the old individual subject by way of individual hyperconsumption. Now the

associations or connotations of provincial misery and renunciation, of petty bourgeois impoverishment, of cultural and libidinal immiseration, systematically reinvested in our images of
the urban space of the Second World, are pressed into service
as arguments against socialism and planning, against collective
ownership and what is fantasized as centralization, at the same
time that they serve as powerful stimuli to the peoples of
Eastern Europe to plunge into the freedoms of Western consumption. This is no small ideological achievement in view of
the difficulties, a priori, in staging the collective control over
their destinies by social groups in a negative way and investing
those forms of autonomy with all the fears and anxieties, the
loathing and libidinal dread, which Freud called counterinvest-
ment or anticathexis and that must constitute the central effect
of any successful anti-Utopianism.

This is then also the point at which everything most paradoxical about the spatial form of the antinomy under discussion here becomes vivid and inescapable; our conceptual exhibit comes more sharply into view when we begin to ask
ourselves how it is possible for the most standardized and
uniform social reality in history, by the merest ideological flick
of the thumbnail, the most imperceptible of displacements, to
reemerge as the rich oil-smear sheen of absolute diversity and
of the most unimaginable and unclassifiable forms of human
freedom. Here homogeneity has become heterogeneity, in a
movement complementary to that in which absolute change
turned into absolute stasis, and without the slightest modification of a real history that there was thought to be at an end,
while here it has seemed finally to realize itself.

3

But as might have been expected, the disappearance of Nature
in its traditional form as social space has also stimulated something like a return of the repressed of another kind of Nature

in another dimension of things altogether; not unexpectedly, this reappearance generates paradoxes and perhaps even antinomies that are no doubt symmetrical to the preceding ones, but of a wholly different character and with quite different consequences. For the question of Nature—the problem of the concept of Nature—is lodged deeply at the very heart of two influential and indeed closely related contemporary ideological positionings in the realm of philosophy and also that of doxa more generally. As they are not exactly themselves philosophical movements or schools, one is indeed tempted to describe them rather as something like a new doxa about the positions to be taken on doxa itself—I mean antifoundationalism and its distant gendered cousin antiessentialism. Both in effect turn centrally on the question of Nature, taken first in the sense of an object of scientific research around which a philosophical epistemology can be constructed that guarantees knowledge, and second in the sense of a human nature of which specific varieties can be normatively deduced and ascribed (for in its relationship to the world and being and to nonhuman objects, the doctrine of essences is Aristotelian and can be said to have been discredited and dismantled by the coming into being of those very—modern—epistemologies that it is the task of antifoundationalism to challenge and dismantle in its turn: something that happens most dramatically and paradigmatically in Richard Rorty's *Philosophy and the Mirror of Nature*). Surely the popular subsistence of the term *nature* in both these rather different contexts needs to be factored into the discussion as a significant symptom, if not any ironclad guarantee that the two positions really share the same problematic.

Their kinship can be documented in another way by recalling the now forgotten adventure of philosophical existentialism, whose Sartrean version united both positions in a common polemic—virtually its basic philosophical politics before Marxism and another kind of "politics" came along. For the first great campaign of Sartrean existentialism challenged the notion of nature head-on and affirmed in particular that nothing like an essential human nature existed; that all essences were "constructed," as we might say today; and that any appeal to preexisting conceptions of psychic or characterological or metaphysical norms of that kind was to be met with alertness and suspicion, the *norm*—very specifically in its guise as this or that notion of human nature—being from times immemorial that cutting instrument whereby the abnormal and the weak, the womanish, the deviant, or the marginal, the criminal and the pathological, are excised and sundered from the social order grasped as eternal and natural. This great lesson was surely taught us more effectively by Sartre than by Heidegger, to whom it would be difficult to attribute any great concern about such matters; it then develops into a whole dialectic— or better still an arrested dialectic—of self versus other, which finds a rich prolongation in Simone de Beauvoir's feminism on the one hand, and Frantz Fanon's diagnosis of colonialism and race on the other, until, in Foucault, it reaches a kind of stabilization, not to say reification, which creates new paradoxes in its own right. For if this repressive effect of the affirmation of a natural self is taken to be part of an ideological opposition, then a new question swims into being about the nature of that mysterious other term, the Other itself, which leads us into an interminable play of reflections, an endless house of mirrors and optical illusions, in which the quest for some ultimate radical otherness takes precedence over the rather different Sartrean critique of bourgeois normativity. This is why—even though it is proper and even necessary for the great Sartrean attack on the idea of human nature to be renewed and reinvented with every new generation—there seems to be something misguided about slogans such as "antiessentialism" and "antifoundationalism," which imply the conversion of an antinormative bias or philosophical habit into a kind of norm in its own right and a brand-new philosophical position wide open to the objection that it has itself become something of a dogmatic foundation and has come to imply something of a new kind of human essence in its turn. But this facile objection, while no doubt true, does not seem to me as interesting as other perspectives on these new philosophical values, which raise questions of their historical conditions of possibility.

Indeed, if following Lyotard's luminous formula, we accustom ourselves to thinking of both strategies not so much as philosophical stances as rather in terms of desires—the desire called antifoundationalism, the desire called antiessentialism—we will be better able to bracket the content of such positions provisionally and to turn to the more historically interesting question of why intellectual or social strata in contemporary society have found the new ethical doxa congenial and useful. This is the only question that can lead us to any increase in collective self-knowledge.

Indeed, it is by way of cognate "desires" in aesthetics that we can best grasp the specificity of this philosophical ambition to live dangerously, as Nietzsche might put it; to try to think without backup or presuppositions, to deal with problems ad hoc and without a system. In aesthetics, all this—which will look rather different—can be said to take the form of the ideal of the "pure" work of art, the work that is nothing but form and has somehow absorbed or expunged everything that was content. "What strikes me as beautiful, what I would like to write," cried Flaubert in a famous letter to Louise Colet, "is a book about nothing, a book with no external links, which would hold itself together by the sheer internal force of its style, just as the earth hangs in the air without anything holding it up, a book that would have virtually no subject matter or at least where the subject would be virtually invisible, if that is conceivable. The most beautiful works are those that contain the least matter . . ." (January 16, 1852). Everything depends in that case on what matter or "content" is thought to mean in this new aesthetic situation, which is henceforth that of modernism; and why its presence in the work, its persistence in the work, would be felt to be an artistic flaw or blemish, traces whose forensic removal sets a whole new aesthetic agenda. A complete answer to these questions would lead us to the very heart of modernism itself, and to some fuller assessment of characteristic artifacts such as the great freestanding syntax of a Mallarméan sentence that becomes a complete and self-sufficient thing in its own right, or the transparency of Miesian constructions in which there subsists as the barest shadow or momentarily glimpsed opacity the distilled remnant and Platonic afterimage of wall or frame. Not innovation but rather prohibition, and the production of ever more stringent taboos and methodological procedures, is the key to this teleology of the modern and in particular the emergence of a specific prohibition that seems to aim among other things at content in general.

A prophetic clue to the deeper sources of this kind of modernist prohibition is to be found in Lukács's *Theory of the Novel,* which turns on the form-problems generated by the different kinds of social content that the novel must process as an open or problematic narrative; and in particular by those parts of an individual life that are somehow not "meaningful" in themselves and can thus not be assimilated to the formal patterns the novel is capable of achieving: never mind whether the diagnosis is circular, and *meaningful* here simply designating what cannot be made to fold into the novel as a form. What Lukács's discussion leads us to is a conception of "content" as the brute fact of contingency itself: content is somehow everything that remains contingent in the individual life that a modernist aesthetics seeks to burn away, like slag, in order that some "pure" work or form can emerge from the process. Contingency is however here not yet the absurdity of the various existentialisms, the radically meaningless; rather it is closer to the reflex of Aristotelian self-sufficiency or substance, as the very terms of Flaubert's letter might have warned us—what is meaningful in and of itself, in its own terms, what needs no external or extrinsic explanations—only *that* is the opposite of contingency for the new modernist aesthetic.

Content is therefore precisely that chain of external explanations (including, but not limited to, causality itself) that is the aesthetic mark of contingency in the modernist context; to put it this way is to be able to grasp the modernist impulse as the symbolic anticipation of a unity of individual experience (completely comprehensible in its own terms) whose condition of possibility is the dissolution of the older traditional communities or groups and the emergence of individualism and anomie. Only such isolated individuals, bereft of the older family or village structures in which they were once embedded, can offer the adequate raw material for the pure work, the novel form beyond contingency (and, as Jean Borie suggested in a classic work, such isolated subjectivity is bound to be a male and a bachelor one, since women are in that situation still profoundly context-bound). Later on, when the public is itself drawn into the analysis, this diagnosis is inflected (by Sartre, for example, or by Roland Barthes in *Writing Degree Zero*) in the direction of the signals and codes that make a work available and accessible to one particular group, thereby excluding the others: content is thus here seen as the mark of belonging to a specific group or class, and the dream of a work without content is a Utopian one, in which the pure work—now something like Barthes's white or bleached writing—can function classlessly and in a universal fashion.

This is the context in which it seems suggestive and enlightening to replace the philosophical project—a postmodern rather than a specifically modern one, to be sure—of doing without foundations and essences. The equivalent of "content" in the aesthetic sense might be located, for philosophical discourse, in those "absolute presuppositions" that R. G. Collingwood identified as philosophy's task, in any era, to excavate and to foreground. The advantage of this particular way of defining the formal issue lies in the still relatively traditional (or modern) way Collingwood grasped his absolute presuppositions: namely, that it could not or never be a question of doing away with them, that all thought and action were grounded on such deep ideologies, beliefs, or paradigms and epistemes, which it was the task of the philosopher to draw up into the light and to articulate, thereby in some sense offering their apologia and their ideological defense. But to put it in these terms is already to encourage a more vanguard philosophical attitude in which the obvious next step would be to get rid of such presuppositions altogether, very much in an Enlightenment spirit of doing away with the sheer superstition of inherited ideas and attitudes.

This is then a move that can be seen gradually to emerge in philosophical modernism as such (if we can identify it as that), for which it comes gradually to be felt—from Nietzsche to phenomenology, from Wittgenstein to the pragmatists—that something would be achieved if one could travel light, leave those suitcases behind, do without the cumbersome foreign bodies of our inherited or unconscious presuppositions: the dregs or lees in the wine, the stuff in your pockets, the houses you own, and the bills you still have to pay. Rorty's antifoundationalism is postmodern above all in the way in which it formalizes these tendencies and concentrates them (with an emblematic identification of Wittgenstein and Heidegger, Dewey and Derrida, as specific forebears) in the coherent twin program of doing away with the analysis of subjectivity as such and also with the related conception of the philosophical system. His work, however, still implies that, as Collingwood thought, you could write a history of the emergence of such "presuppositions" as the way in which, with Kant, the conception of the subject retroactively makes the "history of philosophy" (for Rorty, an error and an ideology that presupposes essential continuities in philosophical discussion down through the ages) possible; but he is oddly evasive about the way one would write this kind of philosophical history—a synchronic history of the conditions of possibility of illusions, rather than Kant's diachronic one—and in this he is as ambiguous as Collingwood himself, about whom it is difficult to decide whether the philosopher who knows about absolute presuppositions does not suddenly in all lucidity mutate into a historian rather than yet another mere mouthpiece for the absolute presuppositions of his own age (but perhaps those were historicist in the first place).

The development from a modern to a postmodern philosophical position, from pragmatists like Dewey, who still have a kind of system or method, even if it is only called that of "problem-solving," to Rorty's attempt to distance himself from the philosophical institution altogether, offers a trajectory that can be read in social terms as a movement toward the ever greater individuations of a new decentered individual subject in postmodernity.

For in an older period—Victorian or Third Republic—such efforts at freeing thought from its "content"—Yeats's "balloon of the mind" straining for release and to cut its moorings with what grounds it—has to do with the elimination of the vestigial content of an older prebourgeois life mode, and is at one with the "modernizations" of the Enlightenment program to dismantle the priests' schools in the countryside and retrain the stubborn mentalities of the peasants. And this, very much in the Enlightenment spirit: for in a situation in which, as Arno Mayer has taught us, modernization and the bourgeoisie are very far from being hegemonic socially, religion remains the symbol of the imprisonment of consciousness in its own past and "the spiritual" is still seen as something like the matter in which modern consciousness remains entangled.

The existential moment is in all of its forms a later version of this program, but in a new social situation in which an even more advanced vision of industrial organization and of working-class democracy has appeared, for which even mid-dle-class enlightenment has come to be felt as a set of presuppositions and prejudices themselves to be demystified and extirpated. In this period (as Sartre's own trajectory from existentialism to Marxism demonstrates), the dialectic is identified as a kind of form that is at one with its content and that can achieve a kind of universality on the basis of its elimination of the "content" of classes and groups.

The "end of history" thesis, which has been advanced to explain why this is no longer our own historical situation, seems to me a symptom of a development in which the dialectic has suffered the fate of all other philosophical or ideological concepts in the postmodern period, about which the related "end of ideology" holds to the degree to which all those conceptual presuppositions and that mental ballast often identified as "ideology" no longer seem to be the principal way in which the social order reproduces itself or polices and legitimates its operative structures. If, as Adorno came to think, current society reproduces itself by way of practices and habits, and technocracy and consumerism not only no longer require ideational grounding but aim precisely to eliminate the last vestiges of distance implicit in ideas and concepts as such—if in other words some thoroughgoing postmodern positivism (that no longer looks very much like its Third-Republic grandfather) has taken the place of philosophical and ideological legitimation today—then ideological critique loses its mission, and the tracking down and correction of intellectual error is a less urgent ideological and political activity than the elimination of philosophical activity altogether.

As in Tafuri's suspicious reading of the modernist moment of demystification and ideology critique, of the "hermeneutic of suspicion" itself, as the "ruse of reason" of a corporate capitalism that needs to abolish the residues of an intellectual as well as a social past, so here too we may venture a reading of postmodern antifoundationalism as a strategy that replicates the dynamic of late positivist capitalism, however much it may wish to subvert it in other ways. It then becomes tempting to return to our spatial and urban analogies and to see in a certain desire called antifoundationalism a dynamic not unlike that of so-called post-Fordism in economic production and marketing, and in particular in the drive to liquidate inventories as such.

Theories of post-Fordism in effect try to come at the modifications of industrial production wrought today by cybernetics and computerization by way of an account of the new flexibility of the product that these technologies enable. Ford supplied a universal product, to be sure, but it was inflexible and the masses Fordism admitted to consumption were obliged to consume the self-same identical black automobile, just as later on in a more international career, the Fordist moment of capitalism imposed the selfsame Western goods on all kinds of foreign markets not necessarily culturally attuned to that particular consumption. In post-Fordism, however, as well as in what has widely come to be called postmodern marketing, cybernetic and information techniques allow the product minimally to be tailored to its consumers' cultural needs and specifications; at the same time the same communications technologies allow a system of supply that can liquidate the physical stock that not only takes up valuable real estate space but also threatens to become outmoded in a rapidly changing fashion situation. These new developments have also been helpful ideologically, for they allow the emphasis to be shifted from production as such (and it would be worth exploring the argument that productivity can now be seen as being at one with an older, essentially modern form of industrial production that is now outmoded); they also blur the distinction between the two other categories of the triad, distribution and consumption, in such a way that new modes of distribution (the fundamental defining trait of post-Fordism as a concept) can be parlayed into a rhetoric of consumption and of the market as an ideological value.

In any case, the post-Fordist vision of plurality and distribution—particularly insofar as it rises above the antiquated and expensive spaces of warehouses and those older storage buildings and display outlets that slow down land speculation and betray the residues of the site and grounding of a more traditional city—seems peculiarly consonant with the more intellectual mobility and strategic erasure of an antifoundational ideal, in its vision of a mind unfurnished with first principles that can grapple with the business at hand directly, in an unmediated and technocratic way, without prejudice or mental inventory or cumbersome ideological stock.

This is not to suggest that post-Fordism is any more workable or ultimately noncontradictory in the intellectual realm than it is in late capitalism as such; for the question of content does not go away and indeed poses itself with renewed poignancy for a liberalism or a social democracy historically obliged once again to confront something it can only identify as a type of fascism. It is a philosophical issue that goes at least as far back as Sartrean existentialism, which, having eliminated essences and human nature, and, although still a philosophical system, having achieved something of the status of an antifoundationalism *avant la lettre,* then urgently needed to show why the free choice of heroic fascism as a form of commitment (or *engagement*) would not be as philosophically tenable as anything else.

Most of the classic existential "solutions" were, of course, modified Kantian ones: the idea of the categorical imperative indeed gives us the supreme example of a formalism that attempts to endow itself with content by taking its own form as the very allegory of the ethical stance to be preferred. Thus, in Kant, the conception of a moral law is construed to imply universality and thus the requirement to treat the other as I would myself; in Sartre (or at least in the first attempt at a Sartrean ethic) the fact of freedom is construed as entailing some fundamental recognition of the other's freedom, which in turn excludes a whole range of conducts (such as fascism or domination); in Habermas the primacy of the communicational circuit is construed as implying some first fundamental acknowledgement of the necessity of communication as such and thereby that of the attempt to understand my interlocutor in a mode of equality; in Laclau and Mouffe the mobility of possible intergroup signifiers is construed as implying the repudiation of any specific content associated with a single group and thereby as constituting a kind of acknowledgement of the very dynamic of political democracy. In all these cases, however, it is a profoundly formalist stance that determines the strategy of the solution itself, which cannot lie in the area of concrete content—of the historical situation, of the values of concrete groups, of specific choices—and is thereby necessarily transferred to the more logical operation of deducing something that looks like content (a substantive ethics or politics) from specifically formal features of the philosophical concept itself.

A wholly different strategy can be observed, by contrast, in Lukács's *History and Class Consciousness,* where the philosophical and conceptual definition—the opposition between commodification in the subject (bourgeois knowledge) and the commodification of the object—is socially identified, and the concrete form of a self-consciousness of commodification is matched up with a specific social class, namely the industrial proletariat. In J.-F. Lyotard's *Economie libidinale,* on the contrary, the opposite strategy is blurted out, and not without a certain deliberate provocation it is scandalously affirmed that all desires and political positions are "libidinally equal." In other systems a structural difference between left and right is proposed, whereby (as in Deleuze and Guattari, for example) right-wing desire is characterized as paranoid, while revolutionary desire is characterized as schizophrenic; but most of these differential solutions will run the risk of seeming rigged in advance. My own "solution," often taken to be as scandalous as that of Lyotard, affirms the Utopian character of all collective experience (including those of fascism and the various racisms) but stresses the requirement of an existential choice of solidarity with a specific concrete group: on this nonformalist view, therefore, the social solidarity must precede the ethicopolitical choice and cannot be deduced from it.

Of these various solutions, Lukács's—particularly if one stresses the kinship with the view of the novel described above—comes closest to a dialectical nonformalism, in which a certain harmony is posited between a specific social content and the fullest development of group or collective structures: a harmony that cannot however simply be chosen in the abstract but that must emerge from concrete historical development. What is important in the present context, however, is not particularly this solution but rather the relationship between the formalist impulse—the formalist temptation, so to speak—and antifoundationalism itself, which is in many ways its supreme form, even though most consequently it achieves its formal purity by abandoning the problem altogether (not unlike Lyotard).

For surely the only logical way for a genuine neopragmatism to deal with the problem of qualitative theoretical tests for group ethics or politics is to abandon this particular longing as an abstract and a false problem, and to deal with each issue on its merits and in its context (if such a thing is conceivable); yet Rorty has also frequently tried to suggest some deeper ideological kinship between his own philosophical views and a kind of liberalism or social democracy in politics. He can perhaps demonstrate the kinship between this or that "foundationalism" and this or that non- or antiliberal politics; but it is hard to see how he could achieve the inverse, positive affirmation without recourse to the kind of formalist strategy I have been describing.

As for antiessentialism, it has also known an analogous alternation between form and content, particularly in the various feminist positions, as they alternate between a feminist essentialism (whether "strategic" or not)—women as radically different from men in their subjectivity and their *écriture,* in their modes of feeling and capacities for action—and an antiessentialist egalitarianism that aims at destroying what is prejudicially affirmed as being unique to women in order to achieve a gender-blind and democratic social equality. But as Paul Smith has argued, feminism presents the philosophical interest of an ideological field in which this opposition cannot be solved and in which neither of these positions can ever be abandoned without political and social loss: women do have unique experience that cannot be suppressed without a general loss of historical content for everyone, while just as clearly the demand for equality cannot be abandoned either. Diana Fuss has therefore argued that an alternation between these positions is as desirable as it is inevitable; while Paul Smith has more judiciously suggested that both must be maintained simultaneously (for some reason, neither of these writers has recourse to the dialectic). It would therefore be wrong to imagine that feminism can ever be an exclusively antiessentialist movement; meanwhile, it is tempting to wonder whether some such asymmetrical coexistence as the one Smith suggests, some rigorous impurity and contamination by the external and by content at the heart of a seemingly absolute formalist enterprise, might not also be invented for antifoundationalism itself.

If such a configuration were possible, however, it would only be conceivable on the basis of the antinomy associated with antifoundationalism, which it was the task of this section to outline, but whose other term we have not yet reached until now. We have however been preparing for its emergence by insisting on the systematic obliteration of the "natural" from postmodernity generally: not merely the reorganization of traditional agriculture into industrial production but also the keen awareness of the age that identities and traditions, far from being natural, are "constructed." Indeed, informational technology has shown a subtle and far-reaching sensitivity for the nonnatural and arbitrary structure of signs and symbols, messages, thoughts, values, cultural expressions, emotions, and feelings—in short, for everything that makes up a human world behind which the material passivities and resistances of an older natural one have mostly been effaced. Nature is thus surely the great enemy of any antifoundationalism or antiessentialism: the strong final term and content of whatever essence or axiomatic, whatever ultimate presupposition or metaphysic, whatever limit or fate may be posited. To do away with the last remnants of nature and with the natural as such is surely the secret dream and longing of all contemporary or postcontemporary, postmodern, thought—even though it is a dream the latter dreams with the secret proviso that "nature" never really existed in the first place anyhow.

This is then the moment at which it becomes obligatory to observe that postmodernity is also the moment of a host of remarkable and dramatic "revivals" of nature, which are anything but returns of the repressed in coded or symptomatic senses. I omit feminism and religious fundamentalism from this account, since both can be shown to be postmodern in more complicated ways, and any reaffirmation of nature or of metaphysics and tradition either may occasionally make is always completed with a paradoxically postmodern lucidity as to the utterly constructed character of both those things. But surely ecology is another matter entirely; and while its rediscovery and reaffirmation of the limits of nature is postmodern to the degree to which it repudiates the modernism of modernization and of the productivist ethos that accompanied an earlier moment of capitalism, it must also equally refuse the implied Prometheanism of any conception of Nature itself, the Other of human history, as somehow humanly constructed. How antifoundationalism can thus coexist with the passionate ecological revival of a sense of Nature is the essential mystery at the heart of what I take to be a fundamental antinomy of the postmodern; that it does so I have no doubt, and one can observe this active coexistence everywhere around us. But it is not necessarily an innocent coexistence, as I will try to show, without at all wishing to place in jeopardy the truths ecology has rediscovered or to minimize the therapeutic anxieties that our catastrophic relations with the planet have finally awakened.

What we need to know first of all is whether this particular Nature, whose violent modifications has finally made us grasp the aggressivity of industrial capitalism and modernization generally, is in any way to be thought of as somehow the same as that older "nature" at whose domestication if not liquidation all Enlightenment and post-Enlightenment thought so diligently worked. The Adorno/Horkheimer *Dialectic of Enlightenment* seems to affirm this, in a well-nigh ecological and postmodern way, but not without jettisoning science in general in its wake, and leaving the status of social revolution and systemic change—still intermittently celebrated in that work—in some doubt. What can lie beyond what Marx called *naturwüchsige* modes of production, if not simply more capitalism albeit of a more technologically sophisticated and globalized variety? Then too there is a second question about the word *nature,* namely, the degree to which (as has already been suggested above) it somehow necessarily also entails a conception of a *human* nature, which may not be enunciated as such but is bound to be implicit in that inevitable and concomitant conception of limits that is difficult to separate from an ecological *ethos.* Notions of a new kind of post-AIDS self-restraint, of a discipline necessarily directed toward the self and its desires and impulses; the learning of new habits of smallness, frugality, modesty, and the like; a kind of respect for otherness that sets a barrier to gratification—these are some of the ethical ideas and figures in terms of which new attitudes toward the individual and the collective self are proposed by a (postmodern) ecology. They need to be historically compared to the kind of Prometheanism and productionism of the modern period, as well as to the rhetoric of desire and absolute gratification that was particularly strongly expressed at its end in the 1960s and early 1970s, in order to appreciate the degree to which the new ethos can also be interpreted in terms of a necessary repression of desire, a self-policing attitude toward drives and instinctual gratification, a new style of restraint and ironic modesty and skepticism about the collective ambitions that had hitherto expressed themselves in Promethean Utopianism and across a very wide span of different kinds of revolutionary politics.

It is important to identify this repressive dimension of the contemporary ecological ethic, about which it does not particularly matter whether it is voluntary and self-administered or not (or perhaps one should suggest that it is far worse if it *is* voluntary and self-administered), in order to grasp the kinship between a politics most of us feel to be positive and ideologically desirable and one we may feel rather differently about, namely contemporary authoritarianism.

For we evidently needed to wait for the collapse of what Jeane Kirkpatrick quaintly called the "totalitarian" regimes to be able to measure the degree to which virtually all the others, very specifically including most of the parliamentary democracies, fall into her category of the merely "authoritarian." A general pessimism, political apathy, the failure of the welfare state or of the various social democracies—all can be enlisted as causes in a general consent to the necessity for law-and-order regimes everywhere, about which it is widely supposed that it is the universal rise in social violence that largely justifies them (even though this "criminality" is itself a response to the failures of the same state for whose rearmament it offers the basic pretext). What distinguishes democracies from nondemocracies in the current, well-nigh universal regime of the authoritarian state is precisely the passive acquiescence offered by the apathy of the citizens of the former: the

whole standing as a kind of textbook illustration of Samuel
Huntington's dictum that it is impossible for the state to
function in circumstances of excessive democracy and popular
participation.

   I want to suggest that these purely political and social
developments are also accompanied by a recrudescence of
naturalism and in particular of older ideologies of human
nature as such: so that it is historically fitting—as incongruous
as that may otherwise seem—that they should chronologically
accompany the awakening of an ecological politics equally
committed to a revival of the concept *Nature.* For the authoritarian regimes today are based on at least a grudging consent,
a deep instinctive feeling that law and order must be the first
priority, along with "fiscal restraint," and that a certain firm-
ness is necessary—that it is worth buying a prosperity inseparable from order at the price of political freedoms of more
participatory and also anarcho-libidinal kinds; that, while we
have lost all belief in charismatic leaders, we are also willing
to shed our earlier anti-authoritarianism and to learn to be
obedient to the most unprepossessing and improbable political
officials. Such regimes, which it may not be inappropriate to
characterize as neo-Confucian, not merely for their respect for
order and their practices of obedience but also for their will-
ingness to rethink the relationship between family and morality
and political conditions as such, finally prove to be based on a
renewed conception of human nature as something sinful and
aggressive that demands to be held in check for its own good
(and for that of those who govern it); power here coming to
be justified in the name of a doctrine of the secret will to
power of all ameliorative social movements. Even the left—
certainly the liberal center—has largely capitulated to the
resignation of this disabused view of the human animal, of
which then the 1960s and their aftermath become retroactively
the exemplification and the cause, the proof and the horrible
object lesson: permissiveness, sexual fungibility, drugs, the

repudiation of the family and authority, the purest anarchist enthusiasm for a boundless freedom and for the limitless possibilities of the Utopian condition to which human beings might raise themselves if given half a chance—all that is now read as the fundamental root cause of the disorder, revolt, violence, hatred, social disintegration, and even budgetary excess we now experience and from which the new neo-Confucian naturalism promises to extricate us.

But it is surely the other way round! For it was precisely the failure of the sixties movements that resulted in the return of these older beliefs about the limits and the sinfulness of a mortal human nature. This is not to suggest that any of the political movements that emerged in the 1960s were unflawed: most were excessive, ideological ill-conceived, and poorly executed, with insufficient leadership, dogmatic attitudes, misplaced hopes, characterological deficiencies, let alone the imperfections of the terrain and the overwhelming power of the enemy's productive infrastructure. But the enthusiasm raised by such movements individually and suffusing the period generally was in itself a powerful and objective force whose absolute disappointment could not but have objective consequences in its own right: the ossification of the new states that emerged from the great wars of national liberation, the capitulation of most Western social democratic governments to business as usual, the sinking of the communist regimes of the Brezhnev period into the "era of stagnation"—all this, followed by the reemergence of a new high-tech multinational capital, could not but document the feeling that human beings are incapable of collective achievement or individual change and underwrite a conviction that some essential human nature, of a limited and ungrateful sort, is necessarily to blame for these irreversible setbacks.

So it is that the end of modernism is accompanied not merely by postmodernism but also by a return of the awareness of nature in both senses: ecologically, in the deplorable conditions in which the technological search for profits has left the planet, and humanly, in the disillusionment with people's capacity to change, to act, or to achieve anything substantive in the way of collective praxis.

But it may be self-defeating to insist on the demonic side of this belief in human nature, which knows a more benign and familiar version that may not so often be identified with the more religious form, but that no less posits the human animal as a creature of immeasurable violence that demands domestication and control, and institutions of restraint that offer carrot and stick in equal measure. Indeed, it was not until the reconquest of Eastern Europe revived many of these same arguments and figures, the burden of a rhetoric now some three hundred years old, that we heard again such language about the peaceful effects of trade and commerce, and the role of the market in reducing the great precapitalist passions to manageable needs and demands and in instituting the stabilities of a "civil society" (which is itself little better than a mediated translation of "bürgerliche Gesellschaft"). We must confront these old arguments, as A. O. Hirschman has systematically done, in order to grasp the degree to which market rhetoric generally is also based on a conception of the sinfulness and aggressivity of human nature that can alone be balanced and tamed by an equally natural propensity of human beings to do business and to make money. The market and its arguments are thus something like the final form of this postmodern naturalism: both an essentialism and a foundationalism, the market offers the spectacle of a whole postmodern metaphysic, which contrasts oddly with the desacralization commerce and nascent capitalism were so often thought to have brought to the older feudal society.

But this is surely a foundation like any other, and Rorty is very clear that Kant's attempt to ground epistemology on the limits of the human mind was no less foundational than the Promethean spirit with which his predecessor Descartes launched the whole enterprise. We must therefore remain surprised by the coexistence of these two seemingly incompatible movements of the age: the one implacably hostile to natural remnants and the survival of any forms of naturality, the other only too receptive to a renewed sense of nature and limit, however grounded that may be in defeat and disillusion. My argument will not mean much unless we agree that we postmodern people are capable of entertaining both these attitudes, both these forms of doxa, simultaneously, with no sense of their incongruity, let alone their logical incompatibility. To be sure, it will also carry no conviction if relations of implication (of whatever kind) are made between these positions, which might, for example, be seen as complementing each other—so that antifoundationalism comes into being in specific opposition to the resurgence of the various naturalisms. Or a deeper symptomal link might be argued, in which antifoundationalism is itself an expression of the same disillusionment as the naturalisms have been argued to be. But both these readings seem to me ways of somehow "solving" the antinomy and reducing it to manageable and nonscandalous proportions. Perhaps, at the end of nature, we would do better to intensify it for another moment and to inspect it for signs of paralyzed energies, and as an emblem of enforced stasis, of contraries unable to enter into antagonistic contact and thereby to develop themselves. At any rate, in a final moment antinomies will be detected at the very heart of that stasis itself, in the general repudiation of the political with which postmodernity has so often been reproached (or glorified).

4

Utopia was always an ambiguous ideal, urging some on to desperate and impossible realizations about which it reassured the others that they could never come into being in the first place: so it whipped the passionate and the dogmatic into a frenzy while plunging the liberal lukewarm into an immobilizing intellectual comfort. The result is that those who desire action are able to repudiate the Utopian with the same decisiveness as those who desire no action; the converse obviously also being true.

It would seem that the times are propitious for anti-Utopianism; and, particularly in Eastern Europe, but washing all the way back over the reactionary revisions of the French Revolution that have momentarily gained currency in Western Europe, the critique and diagnosis of the evils of the Utopian impulse has become a boom industry. It is a critique compounded of Edmund Burke and of the nineteenth-century additions (which we have wrongly come to think of as Nietzschean, whereas they represent only the most derivative side of his thought, soaked up from standard counterrevolutionary doxa), in which Jacobinism is seen as a form of *ressentiment* (and most frequently the *ressentiment* of intellectuals) that expresses itself in a rage to destroy. As for Utopia, it is not so secretly supposed to manifest a will to power over all those individuals for whom you are plotting an ironclad collective happiness, and the diagnosis thereby, in most recent times, acquires a bad aesthetic dimension, as most dramatically in Boris Groys's remarkable *Gesamtkunstwerk Stalin,* where the dictator is identified as the greatest of modern Utopians and more specifically as a modernist in state-craft, whose monumental "Soviet Union" is as grand a conception as *Finnegans Wake* or *A la recherche du temps perdu.*

At this point, then, anti-Utopianism meets postmodernism, or at least the implacable postmodern critique of high modernism itself as repressive, totalizing, phallocentric, authoritarian, and redolent of an even more sublime and inhuman hubris than anything Burke could have attributed to his Jacobin contemporaries. This inevitable but genial next step, then, coordinates current political doxa with postcontemporary aesthetic attitudes that have coexisted with the former without ever being completely integrated into a new ideological system. Thus, we find expressed a very old (but hitherto Western) Cold-War and, as we have just seen, market rhetoric about hubris and human sinfulness (our old friend human nature again) rehearsed with a view toward the dangers involved in trying to create anything like a new society from scratch, and vividly warning of the Burkean Jacobinism and the Stalinism implicit and inevitable in any Utopian effort to create a new society, or even in any fantasy of doing so. Socialism takes too many evenings, as Oscar Wilde put it; people cannot stand the sustained demands of the political absolute, their human frailty then calling forth the violence of the Jacobin-Stalinist state as it tried to bully them into sustaining this impossible momentum. Artistic modernism is then the expression of this same will to power in the imaginary, in the absence of state power or of the deed: and Le Corbusier will bully his clients into a healthy and strenuous high-modern life style with much the same obsessive single-mindedness, while, with more subtle Nietzschean dissimulations and indirections, Joyce or Mallarmé will try imperiously to appropriate their readers' existential time by way of a commitment to interminable exegesis and a quasi-religious adulation. Perhaps it is too soon to add that diagnoses like these are most often mirror images, denunciations of *ressentiment* most often flung down by people themselves genuinely eaten away by resentments; all the more is this the case with images of political commitment such as those vehiculated by revolutionary and Utopian sympathies, which seem to have a remarkable power of stimulating guilt feelings in the non- or no longer political people who contemplate them.

On the other hand, I want to go further than this here and to argue—as the fourth of my antinomies—that the most powerful arguments against Utopia are in reality Utopian ones, expressions of a Utopian impulse *qui s'ignore*. If indeed one believes that the Utopian desire is everywhere, and that some individual or pre-individual Freudian libido is enlarged and completed by a realm of social desire, in which the longing for transfigured collective relationships is no less powerful and omnipresent, then it can scarcely be surprising that this particular political unconscious is to be identified even there where it is the most passionately decried and denounced. But that is not exactly the argument I want to make here, since what is everywhere is just about as good as what is nowhere (the inner name, by the way, of our curious topic).

I also want to caution about the facile deployment of the opposition between Utopia and dystopia: these formal or generic concepts, which have become current since science fiction, seem to lend themselves to a relatively simple play of oppositions in which the enemies of Utopia can easily be sorted out from its friends—Orwell being sent over to that corner, Morris to this one, while some of them (Wells himself, for example) spend their whole lives vacillating between the poles like tender and tough, or hawks and doves. The more dramatic intervention comes then when a Deleuze, examining a similar time-honored opposition, in that case called sadism and masochism, unexpectedly concludes that they are not opposites and in reality have nothing to do with each other (the sadist, Deleuze concludes, is not really the one the masochist seeks and would not participate in the latter's game in any very satisfying way; the reverse also being true in the present instance). I should like to disjoin the pair Utopia/dystopia in much the same definitive way (although it is probably a more complicated operation): it is not merely that the pleasures of the nightmare—evil monks, gulags, police states—have little enough to do with the butterfly temperament of great Utopians like Fourier, who are probably not intent on pleasures at all but rather on some other form of gratification.

A little more to the point is the secondary formal observation that the dystopia is generally a narrative, which happens to a specific subject or character, whereas the Utopian text is mostly nonnarrative and, I would like to say, somehow without a subject-position, although to be sure a tourist-observer flickers through its pages and more than a few anecdotes are disengaged. On my view (but in this form it is a mere opinion), the dystopia is always and essentially what in the language of science-fiction criticism is called a "near-future" novel: it tells the story of an imminent disaster—ecology, overpopulation, plague, drought, the stray comet or nuclear accident—waiting to come to pass in our own near future, which is fast-forwarded in the time of the novel (even if that be then subsequently disguised as some repressive society galactic ages away from us). But the Utopian text does not tell a story at all; it describes a mechanism or even a kind of machine, it furnishes a blueprint rather than lingering upon the kinds of human relations that might be found in a Utopian condition or imagining the kinds of living we wish were available in some stable well-nigh permanent availability; although the great Utopians did that too, notoriously (again, like Fourier above all, who is by way of being the compleat Utopist, the Platonic idea of the Utopian imaginer) reaping the occasional pastoral reward of this or that scene, this or that innocent or not-so-innocent pleasure. Mostly, however, they carefully noted down the precise mechanisms whose construction alone would render those relations and pleasures, those scenes, possible. For the ideals of Utopian living involve the imagination in a contradictory project, since they all presumably aim at illustrating and exercizing that much-abused concept of freedom that, virtually by definition and in its very structure, cannot be defined in advance, let alone exemplified: if you know already what your longed-for exercise in a not-yet-existent freedom looks like, then the suspicion arises that it may not really express freedom after all but only repetition; while the fear of projection, of sullying an open future with our own deformed and repressed social habits in the present, is a perpetual threat to the indulgence of fantasies of the future collectivity.

All authentic Utopias have obscurely felt this deeper figural difficulty and structural contradiction, however much their various authors, like Fourier himself, longed to give us a picture of what they thought life really ought to be like (and to watch our sympathetic astonishment and admiration); they have for the most part rigorously restricted their textual production to a very different kind of operation, namely the construction of material mechanisms that would alone enable freedom to come into existence all around them. The mechanism itself has nothing to do with freedom, except to release it; it exists to neutralize what blocks freedom, such as matter, labor, and the requirements of their accompanying human social machinery (such as power, training and discipline, enforcement, habits of obedience, respect, and so forth).

Indeed, qua mechanism, the Utopian machine may be expected to absorb all that unfreedom into itself, to concentrate it where it can best be worked over and controlled: mechanism and the machine always functioning in classical philosophical ideology as somehow the opposite of spirit and freedom, which then equally classically and ideologically becomes characterized in idealistic or spiritualistic terms, so that its rhetoric inevitably tends toward a kind of angelism. Thus the Utopian mechanism by embodying the necessary—labor, constraint, matter—in absolute and concentrated form, by way of its very existence, allows a whole range of freedoms to flourish outside of itself.

It is a process that can be emblematized allegorically by the treatment of the elevator and the city grid in Rem Koolhaas' *Delirious New York,* which poses among other things the problem of Necessity in terms of the component of engineering technology, what has to be included in the building but can neither be made symbolic nor can it be sublimated (as in the sentimentalism of the Hyatt gondola elevators that weightlessly rise and fall in perpetual motion). For Koolhaas, however, that enormous bulk of pipes and wiring that takes up 40 percent of the modern building (and that can only exceptionally be ornamentalized as in the Pompidou Center's exoskeleton) stands as a foreign body unassimilable to praxis or poesis, one that must be dealt with in new ways yet to be invented (what is necessary in the work of art, said Valéry, is what can never be redeemed in value). *Delirious New York* stages one kind of solution on the urban level by designating the invention of the elevator (in mid-nineteenth century) and that of the Manhattan city grid (in the plan of 1811) as mechanisms that concentrate this necessity into a single structure and condense it, like some consolidation of a variety of debts that leaves you only a single bill to pay. These twin vertical and horizontal mechanisms then release all the delirious freedom of New York to develop around themselves: they stand as the price to be paid for matter and materiality (if not mortality itself), the minimum work time, as Marx said, beyond which the "realm of freedom" comes into view. The Utopian text, then, takes such mechanisms as its object of representation, and in that sense counter-texts about terrifying machines—Kafka's infernal machine in *The Penal Colony,* or Platonov's *Foundation Pit*—are structural inversions of Utopia in the strict sense and are formally quite different from the dystopian narrative as such. (The latter may well, however, include the contradiction between its own logic and that of inverted Utopias: as in *1984* where the premise—that no science or real thinking is possible—is contradicted by the sheerly scientific perfection of the anti-Utopian machinery of state surveillance that is then pressed into service as a causal explanation for just that dystopian state of affairs in which no science is possible.)

These mechanisms can reach states of extreme elaboration, as in Fourier's complex series and the astronomical combinations he lays down for them; but they all in one way or another conform to Marx's political program in *Capital*, namely to demonstrate that socialism is not an imagined figment but obeys the laws of nature and is a reality, like mass or energy, like gravity or the table of the elements. What is misleading (and thereby seems anti-Utopian) is Marx's manner of demonstrating this, which involves showing that socialism is already coming into being in the interstices of capitalism itself, as increased cooperative or collective labor, larger and larger impersonal combinations and work or production units, post-individual forms of ownership, and so on (all of which is even truer in our own time than in his); but his objection that the Utopians themselves were not sufficiently concerned with the implementation and realization of their projects is only true politically and not socially or ontologically. Fourier never thought in terms of political revolution, he was indeed profoundly anti-Jacobin in his opinions and could only imagine the intervention of the famous Benefactor in the implementation of the phalanx; yet everything in Fourier is marshalled to demonstrate that Utopianism is in nature, so to speak, and that the various forms of human collectivity from the smallest to the largest imaginable tend by way of their own inner momentum toward an "association" that is somehow the ontological law of the universe. This is therefore at least one sense in which Fourier understood that his representations had to be realistic, had to appeal to Being rather than to imagination, and had to be based on empirically existing phenomena that it only required a new kind of poetic vision to see in the world around us. Marx himself is meanwhile Utopian in precisely the separation of the realms of Necessity and Freedom which has already been referred to, and which sketches out a classic mechanism whereby labor can be reduced drastically and the law of Value (at best, in Marx, an idealistic, fetishistic, spiritualistic principle of "objective appearance or illusion") replaced by more material calculations.

To evoke such Utopian mechanisms, however, where the part of Necessity is invested in whatever ingenious machinery in order to liberate the space that has been emptied and purified of it, is suddenly to recognize another familiar contemporary ideologeme, namely the market itself, the central exhibit in the anti-Utopian arsenal. For the exchange mechanisms of the market very precisely constitute an organization of necessity, a sum of purely mechanical requirements, which, at least according to the theory, is called upon to release freedoms a good deal more delirious than anything Koolhaas's quasi-surrealist manifesto felt able to attribute to New York itself: namely the fulfillment of private life along with the stabilities of representative or parliamentary democracy, law and order, a taming of the human beast, and the lineaments of justice itself. However base the uses of market rhetoric today, and however baleful its effect in places like Eastern Europe, it may be the best policy rather to acknowledge these Utopian dimensions forthrightly, to class market fantasies along with the other glorious Utopian thought-experiments, and thereby in another sense to ensure that all this remains, and is understood to be, merely a not-place and a nowhere. That the celebration of late capitalism is obliged to pass by way of the figuration of its opposite number, Utopian discourse, and to use the weapons of its arch adversary in order to glorify itself and spread its very different message, is a first consequence of the antinomy I had it in mind to outline here.

But that antinomy can also be approached by way of the critique of Utopias; and it is perhaps worthwhile now to take this path on the other side of things, in order to see whether it does not also lead us back to some central place. To be sure, it is difficult to separate the intellectual repudiation of Utopia, which itself knows an exoteric as well as an esoteric form, from a fear of Utopia, which is a thoroughgoing anxiety in the face of everything we stand to lose in the course of so momentous a transformation that—even in imagination—it can be thought to leave little intact of current passions, habits, practices, and values. Indeed, such anxieties, which are based on the difficulties and paradoxes involved in leaping from one system to a radically different one (even in imagination) go some way toward justifying the charge of *ressentiment* that we have seen leveled against Utopians by the counterrevolutionary tradition: for in fact there is little within our system to motivate so absolute a change, and it is inevitable that the motivations that can be thus isolated, and that link the values present in the old system with the changes presented by the new one, are bound to appear as a wilful lust for destruction and change at any price. In this respect, it is revealing to transfer to the collective level Sartre's luminous outline of the structural difficulties faced by an individual in willing a change from one absolute or originary choice of being to another, and to meditate Sartre's conclusion that, in this situation, the concept of willpower is meaningless. Thus the imagination of Utopia is bound to be a stereoptic affair, which places the Utopian fantasist in two distinct worlds at the same time and generates a unique kind of discomfort by the seemingly irreconcilable demands it makes to disengage absolutely from what is at the same time that one cleaves absolutely to the being of the world as some ultimate limit.

There is, I think, no more pressing task for progressive people in the First World than tirelessly to analyze and diagnose the fear and anxiety before Utopia itself: this relatively introspective and self-critical process need not wait on the emergence of new visions of the future, such as are bound to appear when the outlines of the new global order and its postnational class system have become stabilized. There is a collective therapy to be performed on the victims of depoliticization themselves, a rigorous look at everything we fantasize as mutilating, as privative, as oppressive, as mournful and depressing, about all the available visions of a radical transformation in the social order. My sense is that such feelings, which in their ensemble make up that amorphous yet real and active fact that is anti-Utopianism, do not really spring from profound personal happiness and gratification or fulfillment in the present but serve merely to block the experience of present dissatisfaction in such a way that logically "satisfaction" is the only judgment that can be drawn by a puzzled observer from whom the deeper unconscious evidence has been withheld.

Yet, apart from the political fatigue and demoralization of people today around the world, it is not easy to see what positive values are available to fuel an anti-Utopian market rhetoric: the space into which a postpolitical collectivity is supposed to withdraw—nowadays anachronistically celebrated under the rubric of a civil society that has long since ceased to exist in the advanced capitalist countries—is vacuous and utterly colonized by consumption and its codes and languages. It is a negative result of the fulfillment of Marx's prophecy about increasing collectivization that this process has displaced the last remnants of existential experience in what used to be the private sphere, translating formerly private initiatives into so many allusions to corporate products and so many simulated conducts and desires suggested by advertising images. Traditional images of the family (as of other forms of traditional life) scarcely hold any attraction for the subjects of a postmodernity, who are able to fantasize private life only collectively, as new kinds of tribal networks and organized hobbies, which must, however, in order to distinguish them from other, similar social structures, be marked as nonofficial and nonpublic.

But this precisely sets us on the track of the most powerful drive in contemporary ideology, for which anything labeled as public has become irredeemably tainted, everything that smacks of the institution arouses distaste and repels in a subliminal, well-nigh Pavlovian fashion, anything construed as representing the state and the satellite institutions that surround it is at once marked negatively and vigorously repudiated: something state power itself attempts to recuperate by associating it with American frontier cultural traditions and individualism (with which, given the absolute breaks in contemporary historical experience, it cannot possibly have anything to do save by virtue of images and suggestivity) and thereby endowing it with a national ethos that can be mobilized against other national traditions. But this anti-institutionalism can only secondarily be identified as antisocialist or anti-Stalinist, since the more fundamental object at which it is directed is corporate capitalism itself, with its sterile language and made-up structures, its invented hierarchies and simulated psychologies. This is the only experience people in the West have had of omnipotent and impersonal power structures, and it is an experience over which late capitalism works, far more subtly and shrewdly than any left or populist movements, systematically redirecting such energies against fantasies of "big government" and "bureaucracy," as though the corporations were not themselves the fundamental site of everything bureaucratic in First World capitalist countries. Meanwhile, the positive features of older class bureaucracies—the ethics of service in the great feudal bureaucracies; those of enlightenment in the bourgeois era, such as for the teachers of the Third Republic; those of social service in contemporary America—are systematically vilified and obscured in current propaganda, so that anyone happening upon Max Weber's observation that bureaucracy is the most modern form of social organization can only be stunned and puzzled by so bizarre and perverse a reflection (which comes in any case out of a distant and foreign past). But this is the way in which the hatred of genuinely antisocial and alienated structures such as those of the great corporations today—a revulsion that might ordinarily be expected to fuel the production of properly Utopian meditations and fantasies—is redirected against Utopia itself, where it is accompanied by all the properly Utopian fantasies of gratification and consumption that market society is capable of generating (fantasies about which I have tried to show in *Postmodernism; or, The Cultural Logic of Late Capitalism* that they are themselves anything but materialist in the bodily sense, turning essentially and formally, on reified images of capitalist distribution proper).

As for the more esoteric form taken by the resistance to Utopia, and in particular its more highly intellectualized versions, in which what is at stake are misconceptions of "totalization" and reifications of the theme of power and domination, it is important to reintroduce here the dynamics of the various groups, since unlike corporate or hegemonic propaganda, left or radical theory by definition legitimates itself by the claim to "represent" this or that collectivity (or at least to speak in fellow-traveling sympathy as it were alongside it). This fundamentally collective identification and grounding of the anti-Utopian position already suggests deeper contradictions in such arguments where they are not finally mere echoes of liberal, individualist, antipolitical positions.

An essential seriality of small group politics must also be invoked here, and a serial effect whereby each group, wielding all the while its own specific form of influence and prestigeful intimidation, simultaneously imagines itself to be a minority oppressed by another group (which feels the same way). Thus, to take the most grotesquely illustrative example, the white male majority develops its self-consciousness as a group by way of the feeling that it is an embattled minority tyrannized over by marginals who impose their own cultural values on it. Such plays of mirror reflections and projections clearly call out, not for further analyses of power and domination but rather for a psychopathology of the illusions of power and of the ways in which the media entertain and develop such illusions and projections in a kind of infinite regress (it is a phenomenon Sartre began to describe under the term *seriality* used above).

My own sense is that group politics only begin to evolve in a radical direction when the various groups all arrive at the

common problem and necessity of their strategic interrelation-
ships, something for which any number of historic terms are
available from Gramsci's "historic bloc" through alliance politics to the "popular front" of "marginalities" currently proposed
by "queer theory." Only caricatural memories of specific moments of Stalinism encourage the belief that the concept of
totalization means repressing all these group differences and
reorganizing their former adherents into some ironclad military or party formation for which the time-honored stereotypical adjective always turns out to be "monolithic"; on the
contrary, on any meaningful usage—that is to say, one for
which totalization is a project rather than the word for an
already existent institution—the project necessarily means the
complex negotiation of all these individual differences and has
perhaps best been described, for our generation, by Laclau and
Mouffe in their book, *Hegemony and Socialist Strategy,* which its
authors, however, believe to be directed against "totalization"
as such. In any case, nowhere have such dilemmas of intergroup relations and of the agonizing adjustments that blocs
or popular fronts impose been more insistently represented
and reflected upon than in the Utopian tradition, whose high
point in Fourier unfolds a panoply of complex intergroup
articulations of a mathematical density that leaves Laclau and
Mouffe's shorter articulated chains far behind. Fourier's is
then totalization at its most inspired, and on a grand scale (but
see also Kim Stanley Robinson's Mars trilogy, which will
surely be the great political novel of the 1990s and the place in
which the interrelations of the various radical or revolutionary
groups have been most vividly rehearsed for our own time).

More needs to be said, however, about the structural peculiarities of a politics of difference that is also frequently called
the politics of identity: more is at stake here than some
mere definition by negation and the inevitable production of
difference by way of multiple group identities. Rather, I think
it can be affirmed that a politics of difference does not become

possible until a considerable degree of social standardization comes into being, that is to say, until universal identity is largely secured. The genuine, radical difference that holds between Columbus and the peoples he encountered can never be articulated into a politics: at best an enslavement, at worst a genocide, and occasionally something like a compassionate attempt at an impossible tolerance (which is itself a form of patronizing condescension). The social revolution of our time, Marx affirmed, is predicated on the universalization of the feeling of equivalence and the irrepressible demands for equality that such juridical equivalence ends up producing; in this he was joined by all the counterrevolutionary thinkers, who saw one thing clearly, namely that "democracy" in this sense— the radical demand for equality—was the most damaging of all threats to social order as it has been able to be maintained in modern societies. It is on the basis of that Identity alone that Difference can be productively transformed into a political program; whether that program can coordinate the demand for equality with the affirmation of a separatist cultural identity (= difference) remains to be seen. But the reversible dynamics of these binary abstractions are surely not a very promising starting point for such a program.

Now we need to take yet another step further back, and look into the Utopian vocation of the individual small group movements themselves, as they attempt to define themselves against the larger hegemonic structures by identifying what is often imperfectly called a group or collective "identity" in a specific tradition of oppression and in a (necessarily constructed) historical past. It is an identity that must be based fully as much on solidarity as on alienation or oppression, and it necessarily feeds on those images of primitive or tribal cohesion which were however always the spiritual property of the Utopian tradition proper: what was once called "primitive communism," what is refracted out culturally in pictures of the horde or the clan, the *gens,* the village, even the manorial

family—whatever collective structures seem to resist the anomie of the modern industrial state and to offer some negative
and critical power over against the larger and more diffuse
demographies in which the group's current oppression is prac-
ticed.

But this insistence on the value of the small group itself—
which found its first theorist in Rousseau—is the libidinal
fountainhead of all Utopian imagination, whatever theoretical
problems it raises for a reconceptualization of Utopia under
contemporary circumstances (including the critique of Rousseau himself). For it would be illogical to insist on the Utopian
component of other kinds of political passions—the appropria-
tion of a rhetoric of collectivity by fascism or the other
right-wing movements, the identification of those collective
impulses that inform the various mystiques of modern profes-
sionalism, from male bonding all the way to English depart-
ments—without making an equal place for the conscious or
unconscious role of a deeper Utopianism in the dynamics of
small group politics.

Nor does it make much sense to redefine this particular
anti-Utopianism in terms of the historic opposition of anar-
chism to either "the desire called Marx" or the Jacobin tradition (as that has known political embodiment from the French
all the way down to the Soviet revolution), since this very
repudiation of centralism and statism is if anything the purest
expression of the Utopianism it imagines itself to be denounc-
ing. At any rate, enough has been said to justify the conclusion
that any active or operative political anti-Utopianism (those
which are not mere liberalism in disguise) must sooner or later
reveal itself as a vibrant form of Utopianism in its own right.
This is the final form of the antinomy that it has been the aim
of this section to argue.

A first conclusion to be drawn from these exhibits is that a
whole range of current doxa about contemporary thought and

political opinion is not merely feeble but utterly ill-conceived. We are not at all today beyond the old oppositions of left and right, nor is this a period in which all the old alliances and affiliations have been abandoned for new and perhaps more mobile ones; nor is this particular "end of ideology" any more durable than its short-lived avatar in the Eisenhower era, which was followed by the most politicized era in modern American social history. What such characterizations are trying to deal with—where they are not simply and basely manipulated by the intent to neutralize future political possibilities at the source—is rather the paralysis of postmodern thinking by the structure of the antinomy as that has been outlined here, which confronts thought with a static reversal and repetition in which identity turns into difference, and difference back into identity in an unproductive way that can understandably lead some people to abandon theoretical work altogether (and it is equally certain that the present situation has seen a movement of backlash and traditionalism against all the theoretical investigations released by that transition to postmodernity that required such traditional formulations to be reconceptualized in the first place).

I warned at the outset of this exploration that the antinomy is by definition more capable of figuration and representation than the contradiction: which is to say that it is easier to lay out the pattern effects we have offered as our exhibits here qua effects than it is to offer any satisfying account of the causes they must be thought to imply. Everyone surely feels instinctively that these new types of thinking, these new and urgent anomalies in which we are gripped, as in a riptide or galactic time warp, are at one with what we call the postmodern, and that their historic originality has something to do with the mechanisms of late capitalism as such. But this feeling is by way of a preliminary working hypothesis, rather than any substantive conclusion: the way in which the connection might be dramatized—homology, mediation, participation, symptom—is very far from being evident; it leads one naturally enough to some preliminary consideration of the problem itself, as an indirect way of solving something that cannot be mastered head-on.

The analogy with the modern sciences, however, offers a loose way of grasping the representational problem as it were from the outside, in the absence of its resolution: we are told that Newton's laws still hold, after Einstein's conceptual revolution, but that their application has been found to be structurally diminished and to apply to but a small corner, a small room, of the totality that Einstein found the universe to be. Newtonian law would then govern the realm of appearance of our own historical world and lived experience—an objective appearance to be sure, and very far from being mere error or superstition—while Einstein's hypotheses designate something beyond our reach that we can reconstruct only by allowing for the palpable distortion of our own coordinates. This is a lesson in the philosophically correct use of the concept of totality, as something that by definition we cannot know rather than as some privileged form of epistemological authority some people are trying to keep for themselves, with a view toward enslaving others (the old Enlightenment conception of religion). It may be presumed that the prodigious expansion of late capitalism around the globe promotes it to this omnipresent yet unknowable status, as the capital-logicians argued twenty years ago: unless, as a totalizing force that always had its ultimate horizon in the world market (Marx), it always occupied this supreme position we were hitherto simply not capable of grasping as such. How then to coordinate our very limited positions, as individuals or indeed as historical subjects and classes, within a History whose dynamics representationally escape us? The lesson was given as far back as Spinoza, surely the most dramatic of all the thinkers of totality, when he recommended a kind of stoic adjustment, as a part or component, to that immense whole of being or nature of which we are the merest partial reflexes; it was then reinvented by the practical side of Freudian psychoanalysis, not as a cure, but as an adjustment of our self-knowledge in the light of the impossibility of the cure itself—the passionate choice of and cleaving to what Žižek has called the Symptom. Nor is Tolstoy far from this kind of political wisdom when he sardonically shows the greatest of world-historical leaders in the process of running to stay in the same place and affirming the inevitable and the inescapable as though it were precisely their own strategies. Yet none of these visions constitutes a resignation to necessity exactly; each one posits a certain wisdom in this process of epistemological adjustment, from which alone whatever praxis it is given us to exercise may eventually come.

So one may suppose that the acknowledgement of the antinomies of the postmodern is not a self-defeating exercise in futility or nihilism but is bound to have unconscious results, of which we can now guess little. I have already suggested that the thinking of totality itself—the urgent feeling of the presence all around us of some overarching system that we can at least *name*—has the palpable benefit of forcing us to conceive of at least the possibility of other alternate systems, something we can now identify as our old friend Utopian thinking. Of the antinomies, perhaps we can conclude a bit more, namely that their ceaseless alternation between Identity and Difference is to be attributed to a blocked mechanism, whereby in our episteme these categories fail to develop, fail to transform themselves by way of their own interaction, as they have seemed able to do in other moments of the past (and not only in the Hegelian dialectic). If so, that blockage can only have something to do with the absence of any sense of an immediate future and of imaginable change (using this expression in the marked signification Raymond Williams gave to the words *knowable community*): for us time consists in an eternal present and, much further away, an inevitable catastrophe, these two moments showing up distinctly on the registering apparatus without overlapping or transitional stages. It is the next instant of time that falls out; we are like people only able to remember their distant pasts, who have lost the whole dimension of the recent and the most familiar. As much as a cause, indeed, this incapacity to imagine change (which itself must be imagined as the paralysis of one lobe of the collective brain) also stands as the very allegory of the dilemmas we have outlined here: the Identity of a present confronting the immense unthinkable Difference of an impossible future, these two coexisting like eyeballs that each register a different kind of spectrum. It is a situation that endows the waiting with a kind of breathlessness, as we listen for the missing next tick of the clock, the absent first step of renewed praxis.

Utopia, Modernism, and Death

That there is a Third World literature or culture has frequently, and probably abusively, been said or implied; that the existence of a First World culture follows from this has often been admitted; but that anything like a Second World culture could possibly be conceived of has been ignored, if not passionately repudiated. It seems likely to me, however, that the existence of something like a genuine socialist culture, a socialist literature based on a socialist characterological and pedagogical formation, will increasingly have to be acknowledged, now that socialist institutions and property systems (of which a pseudosocialist culture was supposed to be the merest ideological cover or police directive) have everywhere in the Soviet east been rolled back. We will begin to discover, indeed we are already doing so, that people formed in a nonmarket non-consumer-consumptive society do not think like we do. Indeed, if we resist the temptation (now everywhere resurgent) to attribute such differences to the old stereotypes of nationalism and ethnic peculiarity—here the differences in some properly Slavic *Weltanschauung*—we may well even discover the rudiments and the nascent forms of a new form of socialist culture that is utterly unlike "socialist realism" and intimates some far future of human history the rest of us are not in a position to anticipate.

What human relations might be without commodification, what a life world without advertising might look like, what narratives would model the lives of people empty of the foreign bodies of business and profit—such speculations have been entertained from time immemorial by Utopian fantasists and lend themselves to at least an a priori, external, and purely formalistic characterization. We can, in other words, say what a properly Utopian literature might look like even if we are utterly incapable of writing one ourselves. But the Utopian literature of the past was largely positive, or even affirmative (in a bad Frankfurt-School sense); its "dreams of rest" (Morris) bore all the earmarks of compensation and denial, repressing what its fantasy mechanisms were unable to process, leaving out the negative and the body, suffering and death, as well as everything that cannot be solved in interpersonal relations. But the truth value of fantasy, the epistemological *bon usage* or proper use of daydreaming as an instrument of philosophical speculation, lies precisely in a confrontation with the reality principle itself. The daydream can succeed as a narrative, not by successfully eluding or outwitting the reality principle but rather by grappling with it, like Jacob's angel, and by triumphantly wresting from it what can precisely in our or its own time be dreamt and fantasied as such.

This is perhaps to admit that the deeper truth of the daydream lies in what it reveals of the reality principle as such rather than in what it tells us about our wish fulfillments: since the whole drama of the latter—as Freud and his hysterics taught us—lies in trying to figure out what we really want in the first place. In that case, what we are unable to wish or to bring to the narrative figuration of the daydream or Utopian fantasy is far more significant and symptomatic than the impoverished actually-existing three wishes themselves ("I wish I had some nice sausages for lunch!" "Imbecile: I wish they were hanging from your nose!" and so on). Historically then, this is the sense in which the vocation of Utopia lies in failure; in which its epistemological value lies in the walls it allows us to feel around our minds, the invisible limits it gives us to detect by sheerest induction, the miring of our imaginations in the mode of production itself, the mud of the present age in which the winged Utopian shoes stick, imagining that to be the force of gravity itself. As Louis Marin taught us in his *Utopiques,* the Utopian text really does hold out for us the vivid lesson of what we cannot imagine: only it does so not by imagining it concretely but rather by way of the holes in the text that are our own incapacity to see beyond the epoch and its ideological closures. This is the correlative, the obverse and the negative side, of Marx's great dictum, which informed his theory and his practice for the rest of his life; namely that "the world has long since dreamed of something of which it needs only to become conscious for it to possess it in reality" (Letter to Ruge, September, 1843). Becoming conscious of it, however, is also an objective possibility, a property of reality and of the current situation, and not something to be achieved by will or fiat or by the merest taking of a thought. This is the sense in which the very advances in our own system, late capitalism, interpose themselves between ourselves and the future; but for an addictive culture such as ours it may be more convenient to phrase this in another language and to suggest that it is no easy matter to fantasize ourselves as free of our present addictions, or to imagine a world without the stimulations that make this one livable for us. The attempt at a radically different system releases the imagination and the Utopian fantasy in a radically different way from our own, one that includes different kinds of narrative possibilities. I follow Wallerstein in believing that actually existing socialism was not and could never have been an alternative system, since at any given moment only one world system can hold sway; the various socialisms, rather, were antisystemic movements within the force field of a capitalist world system itself; geared for one form of capitalism, they were largely undone by its unexpected mutation into a different moment, what we now call late capitalism, whose new laws and intensities peremptorily disrupted structures built only to withstand the more primitive pressures of the older moment. What thus obtains was at best the cultural anticipation of new superstructural or formal tendencies, in a situation in which only the provisional sketch of a new base or economic situation can be sustained for a time.

That culture can thus run on ahead and anticipate the forms of future modes of production not yet in existence is a very fundamental implication of the old notion of the uneven interaction of base and superstructure that was not generally drawn until Jacques Attali's book *Noise* (*Bruits*), which asserted not merely the elective affinities between music and economics but also the capacity of music (in the West) to project stages of the socioeconomic not yet concretely developed. But this principle demands two restrictions: first, the mediations are never given in advance, which accounts for the capacity of a form to anticipate future developments in this way (in the example of Attali, such a mediation is at least suggested in the mathematical kinship of economics and music).

Second, the Utopian content of a given text in the present should never be understood as somehow foreclosing or excluding its simultaneous ideological content and function in that same present: science and ideology are in other words not incompatible, but a scientific proposition can at one and the same time be used for ideological purposes, as famously in Kepler or Galileo. Indeed, I want to stress an even more extreme form of this proposition, namely that in a fallen or class society, science, the Utopian, and indeed everything else of value, must also and always simultaneously function as an ideology. There can be no escape from ideology, that is to say from our rationalization of the blood guilt of our own positioning and class situation in this society; the moment of truth is rare enough and fleeting—moments of personal anxiety and of social crisis about which it must also be affirmed that they cannot be retained or built on for any secure and durable kind of truth, although they can of course inflect our practice as such. In this society, therefore, in this history, all truths are also at one and the same time ideological, and should be celebrated with the greatest suspicion and vigilance.

This is also true of those truths formerly called metaphysical; in my opinion, they are to be tracked down and unmasked today (if any survive), not because of some metaphysical vice but rather because they immediately begin to function ideologically as well, and because, in the realm of what is sometimes called spirituality, it is even harder to disentangle truth from ideology than it is on other levels of culture. This is then the sense in which I will want to argue that a philosophy like that of Heidegger is in our time false and ideological, antipolitical when it is not fascist and decisionist, distracting from political commitment when it does not encourage a kind of intoxication of the petty bourgeois ego with its own spurious grandeur, narcissistically obsessed with the self as the vehicle of anxiety rather than with the free acts that generate anxiety as such, inaccessible to other social classes even where it adopts their motifs (as with the peasantry or Ernst Jünger's stance on industrial labor).

But I will also want to argue that Heidegger is true, meta-physically and in some absolute sense, in our relationship to the earth and to our own individual death. Yet that truth is not for us, in this society; here it is "merely" metaphysical, which is to say ideological; it can become true only in a society of the future, in a Utopia in which the function of ideology will have been abolished along with the class divisions from which it springs. We must therefore be very clever in the way in which, today, in this society, we use such anticipatory and Utopian materials as those of Heideggerian metaphysics; we can neither celebrate their truth as such nor can we leave them in the oblivion of metaphysics, which it was their deepest mission to detect and point out. We will return to this exegetical problem in a moment, after making a connection with the previous discussion of Second World literature.

For even if you grant my speculation that anticipatory forms were to have been expected in the literary and cultural production of the Second World, even if you can see how that might be demonstrated a priori and some empty formal descriptions of such Utopian texts worked up in the void and offered at least on the mode of logical possibility, it would obviously be more satisfying to point to a real book and a concrete example. This is unexpectedly what we can now do, as though from out of a time capsule in which works whose existence was largely unexpected, works that express the Utopian energies of the great Soviet cultural revolution of the 1920s and the ferment and excitement, the well-nigh illimit-able formal possibilities, of that period, have suddenly in the last fifteen years emerged in the light of day as though only just written down.

This is the great peasant Utopia, *Chevengur,* composed by Andrei Platonov in the years 1927 and 1928, on the eve of forced collectivization (in fall 1929), and never published. Bits of the novel began to appear in the sixties, a full English translation appeared in 1978, an incomplete Russian version in 1972, and a more complete one only in 1988. Platonov is thus even for Russian readers a new classic, of whom only a few short stories were known in the twenties and thirties. Yet if I understand the situation correctly, he has come in the last ten years to be endowed with extraordinary aesthetic and moral authority—comparable only to the status of Kafka in the West (even though there is otherwise virtually no similarity at all between Kafka and Platonov)—that is to say as a prophetic figure, whose experience is precious and whose forms are historically and psychically symptomatic, a writer whose texts are the object of a well-nigh religious exegesis from a whole range of points of view and interests, whose most minimal jottings and notes are of infinite value, and whose form production, although perhaps less aesthetically realized than the canonical masterpieces of Proust, Joyce, and Mann, or Bely, Mayakovsky, and Blok or Pasternak—and perhaps even constitutively incomplete and fragmentary—offers the occasion for a kind of metaphysical speculation that mere aesthetic objects would scarcely encourage.

Platonov is a great modernist writer, and this characterization now itself effectively complicates our task; since in the West modernism is over and our approach to the older classics of modernism must necessarily be a mediated and a historicist one for which we have as yet worked out few enough historiographic protocols. It does not seem superfluous to add that in the former Soviet Union (although not necessarily in the former Soviet east as a whole) modernism is still alive and continues to coexist with forms of postmodernism as fresh and sassy as anything current in the West. Such "nonsynchronicity of the synchronous" (Bloch) is characteristic of the world system today as a whole, and I would not want it to be understood according to a crude model of stages of development—although it is obvious enough that the presence or absence of a postmodern computerized or media infrastructure plays some part here in the supercession of an older modernist culture or the simulations of a new and postmodern one. One must however also reckon in the intimate relationship between Soviet communism itself and older kinds of cultural and aesthetic values which from our vantage point (and despite the emblematic status of nineteenth-century ballet) may be largely reckoned as modernist in their practice, in ways that have vanished from the habits and the memories of most Western intellectuals. There may thus be advantages to this peculiarly dual situation of Platonov, therefore, as a modernist classic that has never been canonized and reified like all the others, owing to its miraculous publishing history, and to its status as a text first read by the last surviving modernists in world culture, over whose shoulders we postmoderns are still in a position to peer.

But as a matter of fact, the added and unexpected complication of Platonov's modernism is not unrelated to the matter of metaphysics I have mentioned in connection with Heidegger and perhaps complicitous with it in ways that still need to be worked out. For one of the fundamental features of modernism with which it is hard for us to come to terms in a postmodern age is very precisely its trans- or even anti-aesthetic vocation——the will of the great modernist works to be something more than mere art and to transcend a merely decorative and culinary aesthetic, to reach the sphere of what is variously identified as the prophetic or the metaphysical, the visionary or the cosmic, that realm in which aesthetics and ethics, politics and philosophy, religion and pedagogy, all fold together into some supreme vocation. This mission of the modernist form-production, which might today be described, by Luhmann and Habermas, as a kind of de-differentiation, the abolition of the increasing levels of differentiation of a complex modern industrial society, is to be sure in full postmodernism subject to the gravest suspicions and critiques (which I will not outline here, but which seem to me as cogent and pertinent as the modernist project is itself glorious and admirable).

I think we must remain ambivalent about it; but whatever attitude we choose, the historiographic or indeed historicist problematic of a Gadamer or even a Benjamin remains the dilemma, which is that of *Verstehen* or of contact, that of the mode of access to an era whose structure of feeling is at least substantively different from our own. This historicist dilemma poses itself, to be sure, for all the objects of the past; yet paradoxically it is less evident for many that derive from other modes of production than our own. It is perhaps because modernism corresponds to an earlier stage of our own mode of production, the second or monopoly or imperialist stage of a capitalism whose third or multinational informational stage we have now reached—it is perhaps because we have here thus to be with two distinct moments of the same system— that our problem with the past is sharpened and made to seem more paradoxical and even scandalous. That we have such a problem with the modern seems to me however beyond all doubt (in other contexts it is also referred to as the problem of the canon); and I am tempted to adapt Heidegger's reflec- tion on metaphysics itself and to speak of some fundamental repression or forgetting, oblivion, of the question of modern- ism. But the paradox that Heidegger is himself a modernist philosopher, if I may put it that way, suggests or hints at a kind of solution: since as a modernist Heidegger thematizes that forgetfulness of being that is itself forgotten, even as a problem, in the forgetfulness of his modernist philosophy as a whole. It may therefore be possible that the great modernists themselves somehow included, in ways we are as yet unable to detect, a reflection on the very historicist problem that now confronts us, namely the possibility of their own cultural and existential disappearance.

If Platonov survives therefore, in some new and special, as yet untheorized way, in the virtually universal débâcle of the modernist repertoire elsewhere, this survival must itself be- come a problem and a solution all at once. It seems likely, for example, that the very regressive or archaic nature of this Utopia, associated with peasants rather than with the advanced industrial technology of so many of the now utterly old-fashioned futurist urban Utopias of the modern age, has something to do with its actuality for us today, in a virtually completely urban environment from which nature, precapitalist modes of agriculture, and the peasantries themselves have utterly vanished.

This feature would seem to have to do with the more general question of the preconditions, or the conditions of possibility, of the production of a text such as *Chevengur,* which we must now confront more directly. The peasant relationship to the land and the earth is in this text overdetermined or redoubled by the very destruction of the peasant mode of production itself. The dates of its composition (1927–1928) make it clear that *Chevengur* has little enough to do with the enormities of Stalin's forced collectivization, let alone with the terror and the gulag system, which only came into being after this book was completed. It is in fact a historical novel, which begins at what one assumes to be a point slightly prior to the 1917 revolutions themselves, and ends at a point after the implementation of the New Economic Policy in 1923, in a belated Armageddon in which, as in the Norse myths, the Utopian village of Chevengur is utterly destroyed by counter-revolutionary bandits and its entire population slaughtered. This is, one feels, the right but unexpected solution to the difficult problem of how to end the Utopian text; and it underscores the constitutive relationship between this particular Utopia and the violence and suffering that are its preconditions, differing in that from so many traditional Utopian texts that purport somehow to resolve or eliminate the negative as such.

Indeed, the opening of the novel also presupposes suffering as its most fundamental datum: impoverishment is indeed the operation whereby appearance is stripped away from the world

and things, and "the enormous, collapsed natural world" (34/
39*) slowly comes into view as the true ground of Being itself,
a devastated landscape, covered with dying vegetation, full of
chasms and holes, across which human organisms painfully
crawl or creep, or else sit dazed by the experience of existence
itself. This is then a first hermeneutic moment—the laying
clear of the surface, the therapy of destruction, the surgical
removal of the unreal; it is here achieved, not merely by civil
war but above all by the great famines of the war and the crisis
of tsarism, which destroy everything stable and traditional in
an older village life and leave those people who were once its
constituents "free" in the terrible sense of the Western enclo-
sure movement (what Marx describes as the "liberation" of
peasants from the land itself), but also ready to be reassembled
into new forms of collective life, which will find their ultimate
ideal type in the peasant Utopia of Chevengur. The landscape
in which this can happen is then that peculiar, separated,
transitional disposition of the elements as they hover between
two worlds:

> Long was Dvanov's homeward path. He walked among the
> grey sorrow of the cloudy day, and looked into the fall
> earth. The sun bared itself occasionally in the heavens,
> applying its light to the grass, the sand, the dead clay,
> exchanging sensations with them, without the slightest con-
> sciousness. Dvanov liked this silent friendship of the sun,
> and the way it encouraged the earth with its light.
>
> (58/66)

The detached cosmological elements here (whose unconscious,
distracted help for one another is nonetheless oddly characterized as a kind of "silent friendship") anticipate and imitate as

*Page references within the text are first to Anthony Olcott's English version
(Ann Arbor: Ardis, 1978), and then to the Russian original, Andrei Platonov, *Iz-
brannoe* (Minsk: Minsk Universitetskoe, 1989).

over a great distance the relations of the humans themselves, atomized and decollectivized, painfully individuated by disaster and catastrophe, yet turning about each other uncertainly and essaying fitful, as yet undeveloped types of contact.

We have chosen, on the occasion of this unusual text, to associate the questions of modernism, Second World literature, and Utopia; and it is therefore worth recalling the analogies and differences with the moment of emergent modernism in the West and with the catastrophe of modernity, which in truest Weberian fashion dashes traditional structures and lifeways to pieces, sweeps away the sacred, undermines immemorial habits and inherited languages, and leaves the world as a set of raw materials to be reconstructed rationally and in the service of profit and commerce, and to be manipulated and exploited in the form of industrial capitalism. What happens in the West to the existential—the deeper reference of Weberian *Entzauberung* or desacralization—can most instructively be observed in the realm of time, which on the one hand is seized upon in its measurability (the working day, that struggle within the factory for possession of the chronometer or timepiece itself, which Edward Thompson has so vividly described), and on the other becomes the deep bottomless vegetative time of Being itself, no longer draped and covered with myth or inherited religion. It is this new and unadorned experience of time that will generate the first expressions of the modern in the West—in the crucial year 1857, the year of the poems of Baudelaire and of Flaubert's first published novel. Modernization, by stripping away the traditional representations with which human temporality was disguised and domesticated, revealed for one long stark moment the rift in existence through which the unjustifiability of the passing of time could not but be glimpsed, by Baudelaire, who called it *ennui,* the ticking away of the meter still running, the look downward into the meaninglessness of the organic, which does not set you any tasks but only condemns you to go on existing like a plant.

This is the historical situation in which, in modern times, Being could again for a brief instant be deconcealed: it had as its historical condition of possibility the problematization of the older alibis and rationalizations of existence (mostly of a religious type) by the new artificial violence of the industrial age and of money in the form of wage labor. Heidegger does not tell us, I believe, and perhaps he is not interested in such speculations, how one is to imagine the historical conditions of possibility of the "original" metaphysical experiences designated as such by him—I mean the expressions and formulations of the so-called Presocratic philosophers, which nonetheless seem to have emerged from just such a secular break in life experience with the impact of nascent commerce on the elder cultures of Asia Minor.

What one wants to add, however, to the notion of the forgetfulness of being and of the metaphysical question ("why is there something, rather than nothing at all?") is that metaphysics *must* always be forgotten and that it would be intolerable to have to dwell, for any considerable period, within this space of Being in which we have nothing to do but to live the unjustifiability of our existence. Ennui—the organic feeling of our inner vegetal time—wishes to be repressed, denied, ignored, concealed, and finally rationalized out of existence. That great break with nature constituted by the coming of industrial capitalism or Weberian rationalization then at once brings its own myths and palliatives, its own alibis and objective irrealities along with it, to cover over the rift it momentarily opened up. These new and historically original dimensions of concealment, of layers of appearance utterly distinct from existence itself, are of course the profit motive and the new and artificial role of money and abstraction in our societies, as well as the fetishization of commodities, the coming

Utopia, Modernism,

into being of a wall or fold of manufactured objects within which labor is hidden and yet from which it mysteriously emanates with all the mesmerizing fascination of value itself. Western modernism, in aesthetics and philosophy alike, can then, following Heidegger's figure that we have found useful here, be characterized as the repeated attempt to remember, like a word on the tip of the tongue, that inaugural glimpse of Being at once shoveled over by the production of commodities as into a mass grave. (In that sense, then, postmodernism would constitute the moment in which the forgotten memory is definitively extinguished, so that we no longer even remember having forgotten it.)

So it is that in Platonov also the great inaugural experience of secular organic time returns, but within the framework of a devastated peasant landscape rather than in Baudelaire's city: the pulse of this new kind of time is the time of the watchman (lone survivor in an abandoned village):

> After tolling the hours, the watchman still stood at the parvis, admiring the progress of summer. His alarm clock had lost itself in its long counting of time so that in his old age the watchman had begun to feel time as sharply and accurately as grief and happiness. No matter what he did, even when he slept (although in old age life is stronger than sleep—it is vigilant and a matter of the individual minute), as soon as an hour flowed past the watchman felt some sort of alarm or desire, and then he would ring the hour and again calm down.   (9/11)

This peculiar experience of time—*"sauvage"* in Lévi-Strauss's French-literal sense of growing wild in a state of nature, like the burdocks here everywhere across the steppe—is reiterated by the other characters, but refracted through their Utopian diversity and their bizarre characterology, about which we will say something in a moment. So, for example, the hermit, who "had been startled at birth and lived so on into old age, blue eyes on his youthful face" (4/5), perpetually astonished at everything other human beings do. So also the aged Zakhar Pavlovich himself, "his piercing face exhausted to the point of melancholy" (3/3), wandering idly through the world like so many of Platonov's characters; in this case "not unduly interested in anything, not in people or in nature, except for mechanical things of all sorts. Because of this he regarded people and fields with indifferent tenderness, not infringing upon the interests of either" (3/3). Or finally there is the temporal inscription of the protagonist Sasha Dvanov himself, who as a child digs out a hollow by his father's grave to rest: "Papa, they chased me out to beg. Now I'll die soon and come to you. It looks like it's boring for you there alone, and I'm bored" (19/22).

But oddly, it is in things themselves that this human boredom is ultimately the most strikingly invested, as though to substitute for the breakdown of the clocks some new physical medium in which the experiential thing can be measured and perceived. So the heaps of broken and abandoned objects at the very opening of the novel: "There are fringes of decay around old provincial towns. People come here to live straight out of nature" (3/3). But in the great droughts and famines, when the villages are themselves abandoned, the reversal of artificial, man-made, if not industrial objects, to a state of nature is a stark inverted figure of the end of natural existence: a dystopia now not of machines or robots running wild—as the city dweller might fantasize this—but of the peasant horror of the return of the forest itself; here the sudden flowering is not a miracle but a curse, new life means the opposite of the human:

> The wattle fences had also blossomed because of desertion. They were wound through with hops and bindweeds, and some stakes and switches had taken, promising to become

groves if the people didn't return. The wells had dried up and lizards crawled into them freely across the wooden frames, there to rest from the heat and reproduce. Zakhar Pavlovich was also greatly amazed by the senseless event, that the grain in the fields had long since died, while rye, oats, and flax slowly greened on the thatch roofs of the huts, where the goose-foot whispered. They had sprouted from seeds in the thatch. Yellow-green field birds had also moved into the village, living directly in the cleaner parts of the huts, while the sparrows fell from the eaves in clouds, speaking with the wind of their wings their domestic, businesslike songs.

As he passed through the village, Zakhar Pavlovich saw a bast shoe which had also revived without people and found its own fate. It had put out a shoot of red willow, while the rest of its body rotted in the dust and preserved the shade over the rootlets of the future shrub. There was probably a little moister dirt under the shoe, because a number of pale grass blades were struggling to crawl through it. Of all the village things, Zakhar Pavlovich particularly loved bast shoes and horseshoes, and of structures, wells. (9/10)

This remarkable passage gives testimony of the unique nature of Platonov's text, which like all deeply modernist works tends toward a kind of sacred or scriptural status. I will not gloss the bast shoe, with its intimations of the resurrection of the flesh, save to point out the way in which this early passage trains us in a kind of primitive reading of allegorical signs. I will speak in a moment of the impersonality of Platonov's language (not yet, for us, a personal style), of which however it seems important to add the testimony of Russian speakers on its skewed peculiarities, its simple sentences deliberately deformed by peasantlike ungrammaticalities that ground this speech in the earth and in the slow conceptualities of the agricultural classes—and that then in turn warn more sophisticated readers to slow down and to rotate such words before the eyes like natural formations. Modernism, however, has in its very nature to long to be more than itself, more than aesthetic, trans- or anti-aesthetic, to be more than some mere individual work of art whose vocation is to give decorative pleasure and to be consumed; rather to acquire prophetic or sacred status in a social world in which such status no longer exists. So it is that one must read Platonov; Claudel claims that on his deathbed Rimbaud cried out, "They would not believe in me! They didn't have faith in me!" The great modern text in general demands such belief or faith (without always meriting it), and it is this also that inflects all serious commentary on the modern in the direction of the somewhat unctuous and contemplative solemnity of the Heideggerian meditation.

Here, however, in this new Utopian form from out of Second World realities, we find something more dynamic than either the static contemplation of Being or the sterile Western longing of a work of art to be more than mere art but indeed the World itself. For in Platonov this first moment of world-reduction, of the destruction of the idols and the sweeping away of an old world in violence and pain, is itself the precondition for the reconstruction of something else. A first moment of absolute immanence is necessary, the blank slate of absolute peasant immanence or ignorance, before new and undreamed-of sensations and feelings can come into being:

"What are those words called, the ones that can't be understood?" Kopenkin asked modestly. "Dermatology or something?"

"Terminology," Dvanov answered briefly. In his soul he loved ignorance more than culture, for ignorance is a bare field, while culture is a field already grown over with plants, so that nothing else can grow there. It was for that reason that Dvanov was happy that in Russia the revolution

> had weeded absolutely clean the few spots where there had
> been sprouts of culture, while people remained what they
> had always been, fertile space. And Dvanov was in no hurry
> to have anything sown in it. He felt that good soil cannot
> contain itself for long, and would of its own accord push
> forth something absolutely new and valuable, if only the
> winds of war did not carry from Western Europe the seeds
> and spores of capitalistic weeds. (108–109/121)

This is an ignorance before language, an immanence in which
consciousness has not yet found any distance from itself or
formed any concepts:

> Even the most simple concept—for what happiness they
> were living—even that didn't enter into the poor folks'
> heads. Not a single alms-giver knew what faith, hope, or
> love gave strength to their legs on the sandy roads.
>
> (31/36)

This first moment of destruction and sweeping away, then—
what I have elsewhere called the moment of "world reduction"
in Utopian discourse—will then be followed by a process that
it would be too simple and misleading to call reconstruction
or Utopian construction, since in effect it involves the very
effort to find a way to begin imagining Utopia to begin with.
Perhaps in a more Western kind of psychoanalytic language—
with specific reference to the origins of Freudianism in hyste-
ria—we might think of the new onset of the Utopian process
as a kind of desiring to desire, a learning to desire, the
invention of the desire called Utopia in the first place, along
with new rules for the fantasizing or daydreaming of such a
thing—a set of narrative protocols with no precedent in our
previous literary institutions (even if they will have to come to
terms somehow with our previous literary or narrative habits).

and Death

I propose now to follow this process through its various dialectical stages: that is to say, through representational moments that succeed each other by modifying the very rules of the game and the concept of representation itself implicit in each stage. I will first mention machinery itself, since in the passage just cited—and for one very unique character in the opening of this novel—it is precisely "an understanding of machines" that is designated as that "of which the poor were deprived and with which he [Zakhar Pavlovich] was rewarded." Then we will see the way in which the search for socialism or communism is modeled on the fairy tale; and the way in which the characters of this Utopia are grotesques in their peculiar a- or postsocial isolation. The driving force of the Utopian impulse, which is over and over again characterized as a kind of huddling of destitute bodies together for warmth, itself comes next into view. And at that point then the Utopian imagination, the fantasy logic of the Utopian daydream, begins to produce its own internal critique and to undermine the very achievements of the narrative itself: processes that happen disparately and in relatively unrelated ways on the reappearance of something like nonantagonistic contradiction within this Utopia in the form of the lumpens or marginals (here in Platonov's parodic-bureaucratic language called "the miscellaneous").

A second undermining or internal problematization then profiles itself in the form of Platonov's sexuality (and after that in the interesting treatment of women in this novel). These two narrative self-critiques—in which the Utopian imagination challenges its own images as it were and produces new material that makes it impossible fully to receive or accredit the old images and the older narrative lines—these two themes of marginality and sexuality are of course very contemporary and as it were already anticipate the challenges of a new left to an old, as well as the way in which a modernist revolutionary politics has found itself challenged and its paradigms undermined in a postmodern period.

The final heading, however, under which such internal narrative self-critiques can be discussed, is a very old and classical modernist one; indeed, it can be said to recapitulate those very values and principles we postmoderns find most unacceptable and intolerable in high modernism itself, namely Irony, and the quite different challenge an ironic perspective holds out for the very project of a narrative Utopia in the first place. Like all forms of irony, Platonov's in *Chevengur* is undecidable: that is to say, nothing is less certain and more ironic than the question of whether *Chevengur* is to be considered ironic in the first place. But as not merely the Utopian, but also the Modern, stands or falls with this question of irony, it becomes the unavoidable climactic topic in this discussion and obviously is bound in no small measure to determine the fate and status of Second World literature in general today, at a time when this category may itself have come to strike many people as an ironic one. Can socialism only today be described or discussed ironically? Such is then the final issue raised by *Chevengur,* an issue that can of course also be raised in the rather different form of the question of whether irony is itself possible in the postmodern.

Returning now to machinery as such, it seems superfluous to observe that not merely modernism but also the modern Utopian narrative in the West were essentially urban forms and experiences, associated with the industrial city and its new secular social classes; in Russia, as we have seen, it is within a peasant landscape that it must make its way, and by way of violent dislocations that are industrial only in a mediated way, in a semiperipheral country with small but highly concentrated proletarian core areas, within the forcefield of an imperialist world system (the grain markets), and finally under the impact of the most modern, indeed the most futurist, forms of industrial warfare after 1914.

This does not mean that the industrial is omitted from
Platonov's vision. Quite the contrary: it is seen, in a deformed
and visionary perspective, from the peasant standpoint, from
which, indeed, as with so many of the great dialectical over-
leaps of the most archaic into the most advanced, it has a
sharpness not vouchsafed to the Western experience of industry (save in less industrial states; it was for example no accident that the futurist celebration of the machine should erupt
in Italy rather than in England or Germany). Here, the peasant
vision of machinery—identifying its origins in handicraft—is
stylized and magnified as in the distorting glass of obsession.
"The proletariat," we are told, "does not admire nature, but
rather destroys it, with labor" (227/252); meanwhile the character who will in this novel live through and act out the
industrial passion itself begins as a kind of obsessed handyman
and inventor: thinking that "as long as any natural raw material
goes untouched by human hands, people are far from having
invented everything"(3/4). Zakhar Pavlovich

> was able to fix or equip any manner of thing, but himself
> lived life unequipped. Nothing, from frying pan to alarm
> clock had failed in its time to pass through the hands of this
> man. Nor had he ever refused to resole shoes, cast wolf
> shot, or stamp out phony medals to sell at old-fashioned
> country bazaars. But he himself had never made anything,
> neither family nor dwelling . . . He was not unduly inter-
> ested in anything, not in people or nature, except for
> mechanical things of all sorts . . . [And during the great
> famine and drought with which the novel opens] in order
> to forget his hunger, Zakhar Pavlovich worked all the time.
> He taught himself how to make in wood everything he had
> ever made in metal.   (3,4/3,5)

Indeed, it was Zakhar Pavlovich's wooden frying pan—later,
as we shall see, the very emblem of the village of Chevengur

itself—that principally (and justifiably) startled the old hermit I have already mentioned: "Zakhar Pavlovich, though, poured water into the wooden frying pan and succeeded in bringing the water to boil over a slow fire without burning the pan. The hermit was frozen in amazement" (4/5).

This is the character, then, who will discover the futurist excitement of machinery, classically in the form of the railroad: his "body itched happily from the turning of the train's wheels and its rapid breathing, while his eyes grew damp with light tears of sympathy for the engine" (11/13):

> He could sit for hours before the little door of the firebox, where the flame burned. This replaced for him the enormous pleasure of friendship and conversation with people. As he watched the living flame, Zakhar Pavlovich lived himself—within him his head thought, his heart felt, and his entire body quietly enjoyed. Zakhar Pavlovich respected coal, angle iron, all slumbering raw materials and rough-formed pieces, but he really loved and felt only for the finished item, that into which a thing had been made by human labor and as which it would continue to live its independent life.   (27/31)

The story of Zakhar Pavlovich's passion for machinery is then as it were the prologue to this novel, its antechamber, which we leave behind when he becomes disillusioned as to the "general radical improvement" (41/47) to be afforded by machinery or technology proper. It is as though he here abandons his futurist stage, and the void this disappearing passion leaves in him will now be filled by the passion for socialism itself and by the principal narrative line, whose protagonist is Zakhar Pavlovich's foster son, Sasha Dvanov.

It is a fairy-tale narrative in which Sasha and other characters set forth to find that mysterious thing they lack, like the blue flower, which bears the name of "socialism." They

dream of reaching it, without being able to achieve its figuration, much as in the Utopian discourse itself it is a
question of representation in its very content and structure—
the problem of achieving that representation that is to be
the narrative becoming the very narrative process to be realized; this is Sasha daydreaming in the night, with wide-open
eyes:

> Dvanov imagined the darkness above the tundra, where
> people from the warm places of the earth came to live.
> Those people made a little railroad to bring in wood for
> the construction of dwellings, to replace their lost summery
> climate. Dvanov imagined himself as an engineer on that
> timber-hauling line that carried logs to build new towns,
> and he made believe he was doing all the work of an
> engineer—he passed the desolate stages between stations,
> took on water, blew the whistle in the blizzards, braked,
> talked with his assistant and, finally, fell asleep at his desti-
> nation, the shore of the Arctic Ocean. In his sleep he saw
> large trees growing from the pale soil, and there was an
> airy, barely shimmering space around them, and an empty
> road departed patiently into the distance. Dvanov envied
> all of this. He wanted to gather up the trees, air, and road,
> and fit them to himself, so as to have no time to die
> beneath their defense. Dvanov wanted also to remember
> something else, but this effort was greater than memory,
> and his thought disappeared as his consciousness turned in
> sleep, as a bird flies from a wheel as it begins to turn.
>
> (60/68–69)

Nothing is indeed more fascinating and original in Platonov's
novel than this inner psychology of the Utopian process, whose
only apparently subjective movements are here designated
with such economy of line. What marks the purely private
delirium of Dvanov's fever dreams is the implicit obverse of

this: "how boring it had been in the murk of sleep. There hadn't been any people anywhere, and he saw now that there were not many of them in the world" (59/68).

The ultimate Utopian drive, however, whether it be expressed in religious or salvational terms, or in a symbol like the Grail, or here under the magic word *socialism,* seems to have something to do with this recovery of other people; but its difficulty of conception, of formulation and representation, then at once itself comes to be represented by a forgetting— as though the Utopian also were anamnesis, the deep recovery of what is both forgotten and known since before birth. This peculiar impulse then drives people to wake up out of their sound sleep, to make them leave their families and loved ones without warning, setting forth on unplanned journeys (thus Dvanov walking "still farther into the depths of the province . . . [he] did not know where to stop. He thought of the time when water would begin to glisten in the dry uplands. That would be socialism." [65/74]). Indeed, Dvanov's sudden parting from Sonya, early in the novel and after their equally unexpected reunion, is precisely the kind of peculiar and unmotivated action that (along with other, similar events in Platonov's other texts, as we shall see below) will seem to solicit a certain psychoanalytic interpretation.

For the moment, however, it is this remarkable post-Wagnerian account of the Utopian impulse that we will want to trace, from Dvanov's again feverish reawakening:

He began to toss restlessly. He had frightened himself in a dream, thinking that his heart was stopping, and he sat on the floor as he woke up. "But where then is socialism?" Dvanov remembered and peered into the murk of the room, searching for his thing. It seemed to him that he had already found it, but then had wasted it in sleep among these strangers. Dvanov went outside in fear of the punishment to come, hatless and in his socks, saw the dangerous unanswering night, and dashed off through the village into his own distance.   (79/89)

It is a wandering from which he will never return but during which, a few nights later, he will make another, even more peculiar discovery:

> The rare sound of someone's sleeping life rang out, and Dvanov came to. He remembered the case in which he had been carrying rolls for Sonya. In the case there was a mass of fat rolls. Now the case was not to be seen on the stove. Dvanov crawled carefully to the floor and went to look for the case down below. All his spiritual forces were transformed into anguish about the case. He trembled all over in fear of losing it. Dvanov got on all fours and began to frisk the sleeping people, assuming that they hid the case beneath themselves. The sleepers rolled over and only the bare floor lay beneath them. The case didn't turn up anywhere. Dvanov was horrified at his loss and burst into offended tears.   (82/93)

This extraordinary passage is the psychopathology of the Utopian impulse, which demands a Freud of its own and in its own right! The mass of sweet rolls are also socialism; in the deepest unconscious mind the lost object, "petit a," is multiform, the heart's desire is both something so material and domestic as a source of oral gratification and a gift for the beloved and something so complex it stands as the abstraction of everything people have been able to conceive as their ideal of collective life and of the world itself—and all this, feverishly, on the mode of having lost or displaced it, frantically scrabbling among the uncomprehending others, who grunt and curse half asleep at a person seemingly deranged.

This quest will then, over the longer term of the narrative, become formalized into the fairy tale or Proppian string of adventures: Sasha acquires his Sancho Panza in the form of the bolshevik Kopenkin, with his horse Proletarian Strength and his Dulcinea in the shape of a fantasy image of Rosa Luxemburg. Meanwhile, the thing itself will at length take on physical and geographic substance:

> "Where do you come from, looking like that?" Gopner asked.
>
> "From communism. Ever hear of the place?" the visiting man answered.
>
> "What's that, a village named in memory of the future?" The man was cheered that he had a story to tell.
>
> "What do you mean village? You not a Party man or something? There's a place called that, an entire county center. Old style it used to be called Chevengur . . . We've got the end of everything in our town."
>
> "The end of what, for God's sake?" Gopner asked distrustfully.
>
> "All of world history, that's what! What do we need it for?"   (145–46/160–161)

But here the fairy tale and the cartoon or animated film converge, and the Utopian and the grotesque begin to merge together. In the coda, for example, when the bureaucrat from Moscow arrives to judge the village (about which he significantly observes that "there was no executive committee in Chevengur, but there were many happy, *if useless,* people" [310/342, italics mine]), his first glimpse is as follows:

> That morning Serbinov saw a frying pan made of fir wood on a table, and up on a roof there was an iron flag attached to a pole, a flag which could not submit to the wind.
>
>   (308/340)

These are Zahkar Pavlovich's inventions triumphant: in no little consistency with the aesthetic of this ultimate village, that knows no art but that finally ends up erecting monuments to, and statues of, its own citizens, so that you or I, still living, would be likely to confront crude clay idols of ourselves at the turning of a lane. But this vision of art in Utopia (about which Robert C. Elliott warned us long ago that it was always to be considered one of the deepest and surest indices of achieved vision within the Utopian text) is itself a sign of the transformation of human life in Chevengur.

I gloss here a fundamental notion of Adorno's, namely, that what we think of as individuality in the West, and what seems to us somehow to trace the outlines of an essential human nature, is little more than the marks and scars, the violent compressions, resulting from the interiorization by so-called civilized human beings of that instinct for self-preservation without which, in this fallen society or history, we would all be destroyed as surely as those unfortunates who are born without a tactile warning sense of hot and cold, or pain and pleasure, in their secondary nervous systems. "Speculation on the consequences of just such a general removal of the need for a survival instinct (such a removal being then in general what we call Utopia itself) leads us well beyond the bounds of Adorno's social life world and class style (or our own), and into a Utopia of misfits and oddballs, in which the constraints for uniformization and conformity have been removed, and human beings grow wild like plants in a state of nature: not the beings of Thomas More, in whom sociality has been implanted by way of the miracle of the Utopian text, but rather those of the opening of Altman's *Popeye* (or of P.K. Dick's *Clans of the Alphane Moon*), who, no longer fettered by the constraints of a now oppressive sociality, blossom into the neurotics, compulsives, obsessives, paranoids and schizophrenics, whom our society considers sick but who, in a world of true freedom, may make up the flora and fauna of 'human nature' itself."

This is now, with unexpected retrospectivity, the very

Utopia, Modernism,

world of *Chevengur,* whose peasant Utopian figures are all as unique as their individual obsessions, like the man "who considered himself God and knew everything. Following his conviction, he quit plowing and fed himself directly from soil. He always said that since grain comes from the soil, then soil must have its own independent repletion, and all it takes is getting your belly used to it" (66/75). These characters in general, as Platonov tells us more specifically about the party members, do

> not resemble one another. Each face had about it some home-made quality, as though the man had extracted himself from someplace with his own solitary strengths. It is possible to distinguish that kind of face among a thousand faces; a frank face darkened by constant tension, and somewhat distrustful. If these unusual home-made people had been suspected in their time, they would have been destroyed with that same fevered frenzy with which normal children beat monsters and animals, with fear and passionate pleasure.   (142/157)

Like all the great modern novelists, Platonov's work includes an implicit reflection on the very category of the character as such—and thus by secondary implication of the psychic subject: which in all the great moderns in their diverse ways is liberated from the common-sense stereotype of the daily other with characterological properties and features (or "qualities," as Musil's word *Eigenschaften* is translated) and released into the evolution toward that *"fou; monstre incomparable, préférable à tout, que tout être est pour soi-même, et qu'il choie dans son coeur"* (Malraux, *La condition humaine*). In Platonov, this true individual identity, to be reached after the end of individualism, has to do as well with the end of hierarchy ("in those days there was no definite cadre of famous people, so every man felt his own name and meaning" [144/159]) but also with conceptualities, and with uses or the opposite of use (remember that the people of Chevengur were described as useless, if happy, people). So it is that the delegate from Moscow explains to Sasha, about his long-lost sweetheart: "She remembers you. I've noticed that for you here in Chevengur people are like an idea for one another, and you are an idea for her" (320/353). To be unique or grotesque, a cartoon figure, an obsessive, is also, in other words, not to fit into any of the stereotypes of human nature, not to be usable in efficient or instrumental ways; and in this Utopia, in which no one works but the sun, there are no uses to which people can any longer be put ("these adjacent, unknown people, who lived by their solitary laws" [52/60]). These are people "on vacation from imperialism" (179/199), people every one of which "has one profession, and that is their soul. Instead of trade we've set up life" (261/287).

But now we need to look more closely into the origins of this "epoch of rest" in the catastrophic situations and experiences we have mentioned, which here come to include the violence and the barbarism of the civil war. For these two things are at one with each other: "In the morning Shumilin had a hunch that the masses in the province had probably even thought something up, and perhaps even socialism had popped up somewhere unawares, because people had nowhere else to go once they banded together in fear of poverty and the effort of want" (61/69). A page or two later, here is the same idea, namely that "poverty had probably already bunched together on its own accord and set itself up according to socialism" (63/72). Utopia is then here reactive rather than contemplative and metaphysical in some static and absolute sense: it is the collective expression of need in the most immediate form rather than some idle conception of the perfect that can be added on to what is tolerable or even what is not so bad, in order compulsively to take advantage of that to go on to reach some ultimately completed state for its own sake. But this goes a long ways toward explaining anti-Utopianism as well, for the true Utopias of need, of this kind, are thereby marked in their very essence and structure by misery and suffering—they bring it to mind, as it were, at once, they are indistinguishable from the Utopian vision, in an interpenetration greater than any merely punctual association of ideas. Therefore, if one wishes to avoid thinking about suffering and misery, one must also avoid thinking about the Utopian text, which necessarily carries their expression within itself in order to constitute the wish fulfillment of their abolition.

This system of reactions can indeed be generalized into a whole methodological principle whereby the symbolic value of the past and of traumata strongly associated with specific periods forms a system in its own right and generates meaning-effects not always obvious or transparent to outsiders. So it is that a population suffering from the excesses of individualism and an anomie of which they are not always themselves aware will be susceptible to the influence of articulated visions of solidarity and collective life. The converse, however, also clearly holds, so that people who have been "huddling together" for indeterminate periods, such as the various populations of the former Soviet Union, owing to a whole chain of catastrophic situations in which they found themselves, are just as likely to develop a horror of togetherness in everyday situations and a longing for individual privacy and "bourgeois" private life, as they are to acquire categories and habits of collective experience unfamiliar and incomprehensible for the West. Whatever the other complex determinations of anti-Utopianism—and some of them have been touched on in preceding pages—the symbolic effects of such historical and generational experience need to be reckoned in a specifically interpretative fashion, in order to forestall the return of the kind of naturalizing ideology for which collective effort works against the grain of human nature, people are naturally prone to a regression into private life, consumption and the market are more normal and attractive to human beings than the political, and so forth.

But the temptation of cyclical explanations of politization and depolitization is equally ahistorical, and in particular leaves out the historical content of the specific traumas that determine a given social investment: so it is that today the mesmerization by the sheer fact of so-called religious fundamentalism in the Other of the West obscures the origins of this particular collective investment in the various failures of the Left and indeed of modernization as a universal vision. The appearance of some simple, "lawful" oscillation from activism to passivity and back disappears when the specific content of historical hope and failure is restored to a given national trajectory. Thus, for the United States, it can be said that our version of Platonov's "huddling together," the desperate catastrophe that for Americans corresponded to the famine and civil war evoked in the pages of *Chevengur,* was the Great Depression itself. Symbolically, however, the depression had rather different consequences in the American situation: the various collective and reactive attempts to organize a different kind of life in the face of this disaster are somehow reunited in a very different way in the great collective experience of World War II, in many ways the lost Utopia of recent American history and a source of a perpetual nostalgia that can scarcely be harnessed to other political projects, given its association with the military and the "war effort." As for that experience of radical impoverishment and the stripping away of the object world which the United States also experienced in the 1930s, it will be treated by a rather different kind of therapy when in the boom period of 1947–1948, the long wartime shortages come to an end, the accumulating orders for spare parts are finally filled, and all the new postwar products can begin to be marketed. This situation determines a different kind of generational reaction against the trauma of the depression: deprivation comes to be strongly associated with precisely those collective formations that came into being against it, and all become the object of a psychic compensation by way of universal consumption and the surrounding of individual subjects by an immense security blanket of commodities. It is a therapy that obliterates both the crisis and the collective politics that sprang into being to address it, drowning both in the affluence of what is often thought of as sheer private life.

This is the sense in which it is crucial to distinguish the private sphere as that has been theorized by the various bourgeois notions of civil society, and the pathologies of consumption in the United States, and following it, in the advanced countries generally: pathologies that are neither eternal properties of human nature nor inevitable accompaniments of middle-class representative or parliamentary democracies, but rather the results of a specifically unique, historical, North-american experience, that can only be understood in the light of recent U.S. collective history, which is then reified by its apologists and projected out into the rest of the world as a "way of life" and a value, a specific social option in its own right. But this option has as little to do with human nature as does the reaction against it in the post-Eisenhower generation of the 1960s, whose repudiation of this specific reaction against the collective takes the form of the dreaming and acting out of new kinds of social solidarity, against which the present generation has in its turn seemed in full historical reaction. It is, however, in precisely the same way that the current Eastern European anti-Utopianism is to be understood.

It is then particularly remarkable that Platonov should have been capable of inserting, into his Utopian text, precisely such traumas that will later on be appealed to as motives for repudiating it and Utopianism altogether: for it is precisely these two kinds of traumas that make up the arsenal of arguments against social revolution, namely violence itself, and also the repression of the nonclass "identities" of marginality and gender, both of which find unparalleled expression in *Chevengur* and thus have seemed to stamp this particular text as uniquely undecideable and as a narrative to which Utopians and anti-Utopians can appeal alike (we will return to this interpretative problem in conclusion). Both kinds of revolutionary excess are, however, determined by the logic of the separatism of small groups (for separatism is fully as much an issue in the massacre of the middle classes as it is in the emergence of the unclassifiable marginal groups). Separatism, in a formal sense the very precondition for any group reunification, poses the most vivid and tragic dilemmas for any politics that wishes to affirm the primacy of the collective over against the mass-cultural standardizations of a universal privatized Americanization on the one hand, and against the endless tribal and clan warfare of the various nationalisms on the other.

It is this tragic ambiguity that is underscored in *Chevengur* by the ominous silence of the massacre of the so-called "oppressive elements" (in other words the middle-class townspeople and the kulaks), who are "ushered into posthumous life in an organized and healthy fashion" (182/203). We will return later on to this grisly episode; suffice it for the moment to observe the way in which, as everywhere else in Platonov, such atrocities are set down on paper ruthlessly and without comment or pity, indeed in what one is tempted to characterize as a kind of pathological absence or neutralization of human feeling generally. One can imagine political arguments in support of the massacre of the kulaks, and indeed they have been made in the context both of the civil war and of Stalin's forced collectivization (which, as has been said, postdates this particular text), but that is not Platonov's intent or perspective here. Nor can one speak, either, of an ideological blind spot in the text, as has been evoked for the indifference of Thomas More to the persistence of slavery in his Utopian construction: for Platonov scarcely omits the details of the grim complacencies of this virtual execution or class genocide; and there is surely at least an unconscious acknowledgement of blood guilt in the way in which the Utopian group is itself ultimately massacred in just such grisly and thorough fashion—even though that happens in the heat of battle and not, here, as a calculated political decision. The massacre thus comes before us as something like the necessary price to be exacted, not so much for the construction of Utopia as rather for the sheer imagining of it: something transcending in the complexity of its fantasy dynamics that "pistol shot at a concert" as which Stendhal characterized the novel that included politics—closer perhaps to Wyndham Lewis' self-knowledge when he spoke of "paper guns that kill real people": it is the reality principle that all genuine fantasy must awaken if it is to be daydreamed in the first place.

Alongside this, which can no doubt be designated as an antagonistic social contradiction, there are the well-known nonantagonistic ones, which make their appearance with the arrival of a subproletariat, of people who are neither peasants nor industrial workers but what we would today call lumpens, marginals, permanently unemployed, and who in a caricature of the bureaucratic language and categorization of the nascent Soviet Republic are designated simply as "miscellaneous" (*prochie*):

> "Who did you bring us?" Chepurny asked Prokofy. "If that's the proletariat sitting on the mound over there, then how come they won't claim their town, I ask you now?"
>
> "That's proletarians and miscellaneous," Prokofy said. Chepurny was disturbed.
>
> "What miscellaneous? Again the layer of residual swine?"
>
> "What do you think I am, a reptile or a Party member?" Prokofy was already offended. "The miscellaneous are the miscellaneous. Nobody. They're even worse than the proletariat."
>
> "Well, who are they? They had a class father, didn't

they? I ask you now! You didn't pick them up out in the
weeds, did you? A social place, wasn't it?"

"They are your basic disinherited," Prokofy explained.
"They weren't living anywhere, they were wandering."

(226/250–51)

The arrival of the "miscellaneous" (with their ominously "non-
Russian faces" [231/256]) triggers what may with a certain
exaggeration be called class conflict or at least tension within
the classless society, the reemergence of social dynamics and
struggles within Utopia itself. They are compared to "seeds
from some nameless weedpatch" that "fall onto bare clay or by
the empty lands of the earth, and are able to find nourishment
in bare minerals" (231/255). It is worth quoting at some
length Platonov's remarkable evocation of these faceless and
anonymous people:

> Other people had an entire armament to strengthen and
> develop their own valued lives, while the miscellaneous had
> only one weapon with which to cling to this earth, and that
> was the last traces of a mother's warmth within the baby's
> body. This alone however was enough to make the child
> survive, struggle, and arrive in his own future alive. That
> sort of past life had exhausted the strength of those who had
> come to Chevengur, and thus to Chepurny they seemed
> powerless and nonproletarian elements, as though they had
> spent their entire lives basking beneath not the sun, but
> the moon. However, after exhausting their strength in
> preserving the first parental warmth within, fighting against
> the headwind which wished to uproot them, fighting against
> inimical life, and after even multiplying that warmth on
> earnings gleaned from the real people, the people with
> names, the miscellaneous had made of themselves exercises
> in endurance, and within the inner substance of the bodies
> of the miscellaneous had formed minds full of curiosity and

doubt, quick feelings capable of exchanging eternal bliss for a brother comrade who also had no father and no property, but who could make one forget both the one and the other. The miscellaneous still carried hopes within themselves, hopes that were sure, successful, and melancholy as loss itself. The precision of this hope was that if one were to succeed at the main task of remaining live and whole, then all the rest and everything which one might desire would succeed as well, even if that required leading the entire world to its final grave. If however this main task were fulfilled and survived and the prime necessity, which is not happiness but indispensability, was not encountered, then there would not be time enough to find it in the rest of life unlived. After all, there is not enough time to catch that which is lost, or perhaps that which is wasted disappears from the earth entirely. Many of the miscellaneous had walked all of the open, ever-changing roads and had found nothing.   (231/255–6)

Yet this more fundamental anonymity—this rock-bottom of the individual subject that can alone, like the most radical of all chains enable the coming into being of a collective of genuine equality—can also become a source of strength for the Utopia of *Chevengur,* if it is celebrated with the proper Bakhtinian spirit and in anticipation of contemporary or post-modern celebrations of difference; if in other words Chepurny is right to sense "that the Chevengur proletariat desired the international, which is to say distant, foreign and outlandish people, in order to unite with them so that the entire motley life of earth could grow together in one tree" (274/301).

There is something more ineradicably tragic, however, about the arrival of the women in Chevengur, which offers the Soviet or socialist-realist analogue to the obligatory scene in the American Western when finally the wagon loads of whores are driven into the new settlement with its mud streets and

plank sidewalks. Revolutionary puritanism is carefully marked
and set in place in Chepurny's fear of sexuality and his insistence that the women not be beautiful. Despite that, the new
recruits have their own (justifiable) doubts about the new
social order:

> The women were immediately frightened. The former men
> had always begun their business with them right at the end,
> while these held out and waited, giving speeches first. So
> the women pulled the overcoats and greatcoats in which
> Klavdyusha had dressed them right up to their noses, cov-
> ering the openings of their mouths. They were not afraid
> of love, for they did not love, but they did fear torment,
> the near destruction of their bodies by these dry, patient
> men in soldiers' greatcoats, their faces etched by the trials
> of their lives. These women possessed no youth or other
> obvious age. They had exchanged their bodies, their places
> of age and blossoming, for food, and since the procurement
> of food was always unprofitable for them, their bodies were
> expended before their death. Long before it. For that
> reason they resembled both young girls and old women,
> both mothers and younger, undernourished sisters.
>
> (314/346–47)

This specific form of pity in Platonov, whose accents here and
elsewhere are unique, can to be sure be interpreted in a
variety of different ways, whose very variety leads us to what
is most problematical and contradictory in *Chevengur* itself. The
first interpretive option is clearly enough the metaphysical
one, that even in Utopia, organic beings will still suffer:

> "But have you got misery here or sadness here in Chev-
> engur?" Serbinov asked.
> Dvanov told him there was. Misery and sorrow are also the
> body of the human being.   (308/339)

From this perspective Utopia is merely the political and social solution of collective life: it does not do away with the tensions and unresolvable contradictions inherent both in interpersonal relations and in bodily existence itself (among them those of sexuality), but rather exacerbates those and allows them free rein, by removing the artificial miseries of money and self-preservation. The Heideggerian perspective—which grants the achievement of the social Utopia the privilege of deconcealing Being itself—also opens up the experience of death that is at the heart of Being; it is thus no accident that the fundamental moment of doubt the militants have about socialism itself comes after a grotesque scene in which the Chevengurians are unable to bring a sick child back to life (247/272–3). But, of course, it is not the function of Utopia to bring the dead back to life nor to abolish death in the first place; death is so deeply inscribed in this Utopia that it begins and ends with an exemplary suicide:

> Zakhar Pavlovich had known one man, a fisherman from Lake Mutevo, who had questioned many people about death, and was tormented by his curiosity. This fisherman loved fish most of all not as food, but as special beings that definitely knew the secret of death. He would show Zakhar Pavlovich the eyes of a dead fish and say, "Look—there's wisdom! A fish stands between life and death, so that he's dumb and expressionless. I mean even a calf thinks, but a fish, no. It already knows everything." Contemplating the lake through the years, the fisherman thought always about the same thing, about the interest of death. Zakhar Pavlovich tried to talk him out of it, saying, "There's nothing special there, just something tight." After a year the fisherman couldn't stand it any more and threw himself into the lake from his boat, after tying his feet with a rope so that he wouldn't accidentally float. In secret he didn't even believe in death. The important thing was that he wanted

to look at what was there—perhaps it was much more interesting than living in a village or on the shores of a lake. He saw death as another province, located under the heavens as if at the bottom of cool water, and it attracted him. Some of the muzhiks that the fisherman talked with about his intention to live awhile with death and return tried to talk him out of it, but others agreed with him.

"What the hell, Mitry Ivanich, nothing ventured, nothing gained. Try it, then come back and tell us." Dmitry Ivanich tried—they dragged him from the lake after three days and buried him near the fence of the village graveyard.   (6/7)

The protagonist Dvanov, who drowns himself in this lake after the genocide of Chevengur, is the son of this same muzhik, whose morbid curiosity we will want to return to in a different connection in a moment. Yet there is no great inconsistency between Utopia and death, the former being what you do to distract yourself from the organic boredom of the latter.

On a second reading, however, the passages I have quoted, and not only those about the women of Chevengur, are to be read in a fundamentally psychoanalytic way, as a deep and morbid fear of life and of sexuality in Platonov—an interpretation obviously a good deal more difficult to universalize than the preceding one, and yet an interpretive temptation that is very difficult to avoid without the risk of rationalization or repression. The argument about the status of psychoanalytic interpretation and psychoanalytic criticism remains urgent and crucial at the present time, even though its basic terms have been almost completely modified. In the past, it was always necessary to argue for the relevance, not just of one but of many distinct forms of the psychoanalytic—even though success in such an argument then meant the necessity of opening up new connections and relations between the psychoanalytic interpretations thus acquired and all the others, which did not thereby lose any of their own validity. Today, however, psychoanalysis is so widely accepted as to have been emptied of its capacity to scandalize and therapeutically to shock or to defamiliarize, while in the postmodern the very existence of an Unconscious as such has come widely into doubt. Finally the psychoanalytic, as a grounding and a metaphysic that seems unmetaphysical, seems to have begun to function as everyone's fall-back interpretive code in a situation in which we have all pretended to give up "ultimately determining instances" of all the other kinds. Platonov may not afford the best textual situation to argue out these new problems posed by an institutional or canonized psychoanalysis, but they had to be at least mentioned on the occasion of a text in which the horror of sexuality seems to play a scarcely veiled role whose field of influence, however, seems hard enough to determine. The step into the sexual, for example, is isolated from the rest of life in a charged and peculiar manner calculated to produce meaning rather than to be itself interpretable in any simple causal fashion. Thus the inauguration of socialism is fantasized in a way that might be merely figural and decorative in another writer, but that in Platonov is ominous indeed:

> Chepurny sat in fear of the coming day, because that first day would be somehow clumsy and awful, as though something that had always been virginal proved now ripe for marriage, and on the morrow everyone must marry. Chepurny kneaded his face with his hands in his embarrassment, then sat motionless for a long while, enduring his senseless shame. (205/228)

But the relationship to sexuality is crucial because it offers an alternate reason for (and reading of) the quest itself and for the inexplicable departures: suddenly leaving wife or lover behind in the middle of the night (as we have seen), or wandering out into the steppe in a fever in order to discover "the people." Dvanov's departure is underscored by its replay in an even more enigmatic, yet mysteriously significant short story called "Homecoming," whose protagonist is discovered years later in a neighboring town, after just such another abrupt and unexplained departure from family and marriage, cleaning out latrines—as though abnegation of this kind had some distant connection with the most morbid images of sainthood and asceticism. But if it is a psychoanalytic account that is called for here, then both sainthood and socialism are little more than sick rationalizations, and the political or Utopian content of *Chevengur* is thereby fundamentally problematized, if not canceled out.

Yet a third line of interpretation now opens up, which includes this one in some form, but is nonetheless a good deal more universal in its formalisms; this is irony itself, a topic that has significance in a number of contexts including that of modernism, of which it is canonically understood to be the supreme moral and aesthetic achievement and the dominant value. It would not, then, be surprising to be forced into the conclusion that a modernist writer of Platonov's achievements would turn out to include, somewhere, and despite the fact that we are here East rather than West, the fundamental fact of irony; and indeed I think that we will not be able to avoid doing so. But here too the Second World may have something new to teach the First World about a modernist value that is no longer operative or functional within the latter's postmodern stage.

At least five kinds of irony seem to me attributable to Platonov's text: the most superficial and stylistic would surely have to do with the incongruities of a peasant language and a peasant ignorance, from which the sophisticated Russian writer takes some unmeasurable distance here, incalculable not least because, in a well-nigh zero degree of personal style, Platonov has virtually disappeared behind his peasant characters and their language. But this irony—which we may designate as the irony of the intellectual—might itself slip over into a rather different irony, that of the communist militant, contemplating the simple-minded Utopian vagaries of these peasant organizers, who plan, for example, to release their surviving cattle in the name of socialist construction:

> "Pretty soon we're going to turn the livestock out into nature . . . after all, they're almost people. It's just that age-old oppression has made the livestock lag behind man. But the livestock wants to become people too, you know!"   (157/174)

With this not implausible reading *Chevengur* offers an exhaustive description of everything backward and not yet politically conscious in the peasant mentality, as well as something like a balance sheet or agenda of the cultural work socialist construction has before it.

But once achieved, this kind of political reading can easily give way to another, related, but inverted one: the irony of the committed and political anticommunist, for whom *Chevengur* is very precisely a denunciation of socialism and Utopia, and an anatomy of what is repressive about the latter; here the key text would surely be that of the massacre of the bourgeoisie to which I have already alluded, but any number of moments of an awkward or stupid repressive violence will trigger the familiar Sovietological anticommunist readings through which, for the most part, all the Soviet works of any literary quality have been filtered on their transmission to the West.

Nor is it impossible to subsume the psychoanalytic reading I have just mentioned under the larger rubric of irony, as a way of similarly discrediting the political elements and impulses of *Chevengur:* that the quest for socialism should turn out to be a category-mistake and a form of sexual avoidance behavior is as effective a way of depoliticizing history as the Oedipal interpretations of the student revolts of May 1968 or Tiananmen Square.

But in fact the ultimate form that an ironic reading of Chevengur can take lies in its interpretation in terms of irony itself, as some ultimate life stance and moral and political metaphysic. We have indeed not sufficiently commented on the glaciality of Platonov's tone, the ruthlessness with which this narrative sets the most gruesome things in place, without comment, in a dissociation of sensibility so absolute that it sometimes evades our attention altogether like a pane of glass. The massacre is only the most dramatic example of this narration at great distance; we can also observe it happening in the narrative of the experience of individual characters when suddenly, from the outside, we learn that one has fallen ill of a high fever—indeed, has already had a high fever for some time without our knowing it, who have been witnessing events through that character's eyes. The reader is struck by an utter lack of writerly self-consciousness in such passages—quite unlike the contrived omissions of Hemingway or the strategic leaps and shocks in Forster—as though in this case the writer himself did not even notice the difference; as though the events were unfolding before some impersonal registration mechanism that passed no judgement on them and entertained no discernable reaction.

Indeed, we can only become aware of everything that is peculiar about this procedure by a complicated reading operation whereby we ourselves draw back from the data furnished us in order to reconstruct it in a different—and more stereotypical and familiar—recognizable form. We marshall a certain number of gestures and exclamations, put them back together again according to the dictates of common sense, look more closely at the results, and then murmur to ourselves, with no little bemusement: But . . . this is a massacre, these people are being killed! And then, in a second moment, we return to the text to ask ourselves: But is the writer aware of this? does he know what is going on? If this question can be answered in the affirmative, then we have to do in such a passage with what is normally characterized as irony: logical implication is then enough to allow us in yet a third moment to reconstruct an authorial position and judgement that had seemed absent, and to "decide" what the peculiarly neutral passage is in reality supposed to mean. But one of the peculiarities of irony itself in its purest form is that this third step is undecideable and depends on some prior decision of our own in the void; nothing in the text authorizes it, nothing can be adduced after the fact to falsify or verify the interpretation in question.

Recall, for example, the fisherman whose death I have already quoted above. The text, in all its peasant simple-mindedness, tells the story in terms of a fable or a fairy-tale, on the order of the boy who wanted to know fear. Here the fisherman wants to know death, and as in fairy-tales, takes steps to do so; unlike the fairy-tale form, however, no magical or didactic surprises complete the narrative—the fisherman simply drowns, and is then buried. In his film version, Alexander Sokurov adds the fairy-tale structure back in, in a way that makes for an instructive comparison: here it is the son who wants to know death; the father rows him out in the boat, helps him tie up his legs, and later on calls down into the water, asking the boy to tell him what it's like. Here at least we have a kind of closure, which transforms the mere event into an anecdote with a narrative shape. In Platonov's text, the only result is to add the fisherman to the novel's portrait gallery of obsessed lunatics or mentally retarded cretins.

On the other hand, the reader is also free to draw back from the text in the way I have described. Then the fisherman's act slowly reforms into a more recognizable event, namely what we normally call "suicide," into which we reckon back all that mental distress, incurable depression, anguish, intolerable mental suffering that presumably accompany the taking of one's own life; in this textual context, we then selectively test it for plausible inner-worldly motives such as famine, family troubles, or mid-life crisis.

But the realistic common-sense picture of the fisherman's suicide that we reconstruct from this perspective is absolutely incompatible, it seems to me, with the fable about the man who grew more and more curious about death. At this point the only irony that seems plausible is the first of those mentioned, the irony of the sophisticate for the peasant who thinks he is curious about death when in reality he simply wants to commit suicide. Yet even that irony is too strongly positioned; it implies a judgement of Platonov that the eerie blankness and impersonality of this text would seem to exclude. One conjectures therefore a final moment of synthesis beyond irony, in which the two versions of this event are again reconciled, by way of some protoreligious belief in that other, underwater, otherworldly space that might itself somehow be the Utopia of this one: and indeed the text tells us many hundred pages later in passing that

> Communism tormented Chepurny the way the secret of life after death had tormented Dvanov's father. Chepurny could not bear the mystery of time, so he cut short the length of history by the rapid construction of communism in Chevengur, just as the fisherman Dvanov could not bear his own life and so had transformed it into death, in order to experience the beauty of that world.   (259/285).

Unfortunately, this late rationalization or motivation of the episode merely kicks the mechanisms of irony into play all over again, in an interminable vicious circle.

Irony in the West—or in Western high modernism—meant two things, whose very coexistence is itself "ironic." As a literary procedure and a property of the emergent modern novel, it reflected a twofold demographic enlargement: the experience of great masses of people in the industrial city, and the wider sense of a global population brought to the metropolis by way of the new imperialisms. This sudden awareness of the multiplicity of other people coexisting with me determines an existential crisis in the metropolis whose effect is that radical devaluation of individual experience we call irony; it is inscribed in the narrative texts as a multiplicity of narrative perspectives or points of view, which relativize each other's hitherto absolute values. This kind of irony is signed by any number of illustrious names, from Henry James and Conrad across Gide and Fernando Pessoa to Pirandello.

This first, social irony is pressed into the service of a second, more political and ideological kind, which might be subscribed to by names like Thomas Mann but that finds its fullest development in the ideologues of modernism and in particular the Anglo-American literary critics all the way to New Criticism. This second kind of irony, which it might be more appropriate to call antipolitical, finds its vocation in a rather different kind of social and ideological crisis—namely that of the modernist artists and writers themselves, whose mission and talent, along with their very artistic programs, spring from their loathing of the bourgeoisie and their repudiation of a market society, but whose formation largely forbids any serious long-term alliance with the other social class. In this situation of Hegelian Unhappy Consciousness and Sartrean bad faith alike, the second form of irony comes as a solution; for it allows that devaluation of personal experience and values achieved in the first form of irony to be transferred to the political situation, where it can now secure the bracketing of any fundamental personal and political commitment, while enabling the contemplative and henceforth purely aesthetic persistence of an oppositional social stance.

This is the way in which the power of the various aesthetic modernisms was, during the Cold War and in the period of their North American canonization, displaced and invested in essentially antipolitical forms of academic aestheticism. The

arrival of postmodernism, which now allows us to rewrite the
history of modernism itself, may thus also allow us to revise
this now virtually universal stereotype of the great Western
modernists as subjective and quietistic antipolitical figures (a
stereotype that had in any case to be an Anglo-American one,
although its more recent construction in a depoliticized France
suggests that it will in future years have an attraction in other
national traditions at the very moment in which it loses its
credibility for our own).

But this situation explains why irony and Utopia have so
often been felt to be incompatible, and why irony's supreme
mission has indeed often been formulated as that of a weapon
against the Utopian imagination. Platonov forces us to raise
this issue again in a new way, without necessarily having any
new solutions for us. He himself seems to have tried to resolve
it by way of that radical depersonalization and chilling off of
affect that we have referred to several times, and that, in one
of the most remarkable pages of *Chevengur,* becomes a veritable
vision of the dissociation of the self (which is also susceptible
to a rewriting in terms of the religious narratives of the
guardian angel):

But there is within man also a tiny spectator who takes part
neither in action nor in suffering, and who is always cold-
blooded and the same. It is his service to see and be a
witness, but he is without franchise in the life of man and
it is not known why he exists in solitude. This corner of
man's consciousness is lit both day and night, like the
doorman's room in a large building. This heart doorman
sits entire days at the entrance into man and knows all the
inhabitants of his building, but not a single resident asks the
doorman's advice about his affairs. The residents come and
go, while the spectator-doorman watches them with his
eyes. His powerless knowledge of everything makes him
sometimes seem sad, but he is always polite, distant, and

he keeps an apartment in another building. In the event of fire the doorman telephones the firemen and watches further events from without.

While Dvanov walked and rode without memory, this spectator within him saw everything, but it never warned him and never helped him, not once. He lived parallel to Dvanov, but he wasn't Dvanov.

He existed somewhat like a man's dead brother; everything human seemed to be at hand, but something tiny and vital was lacking. Man never remembers him, but always trusts him, just as when a tenant leaves his house and his wife within, he is never jealous of her and the doorman.

This is the eunuch of man's soul. It was to this that he was a witness.   (80/90)

This enigmatic passage (compounded by other strange texts of Platonov that have only recent come to light, which deal even more explicitly with sexuality) leaves us with questions to which only psychoanalysis would seem to have answers (but see Valery Podoroga's remarkable reading of it). Yet it seems important, if not to refuse those particular clinical answers altogether, at least to defer them as long as possible, so that more formal problems have time to be raised if not settled.

Even if this stark depersonalization is grasped as something like a zero-degree and a virtual suicide of modernist irony (as I myself would tend to do), the question of its formal necessity remains open. Indeed, much in Platonov's shorter writing suggests that he required the framework of the larger Utopian narrative to develop an essentially lyric and fragmented content that is otherwise trivialized in shorter texts, when it is not altogether mediocre. Platonov is, to be sure, very far from being the only modern writer to suffer this disjunction of fancy and imagination, of the molecular and the molar, as a well-nigh unresolvable formal crisis that could also, on occasion, be transformed into a more productive form-problem (as Lukács called it), without for all that being transcended. This particular problem, in which the attention to the minutely lyrical is incompatible with plot progression or narrative, is indeed uniquely remotivated by the episodic nature of the Utopian text, which came as a rescue for just such individual lyric moments in Platonov that otherwise had nowhere else to go— unless they were simply to end up allegorically designating themselves as such. Indeed, his greatest single short story, "Homecoming," with the hero's seemingly pathological and unmotivated departure from home and family, his voluntary abandonment of ordinary happiness, may be said allegorically to constitute Platonov's recognition that the lyric present has no destination and no principle of duration; that it must be given up or sacrificed, in order to secure even an unmotivated larger narrative form.

As for a sexual or psychoanalytic explanation of the "eunuch of the soul," it seems important to make this into a two-way street and to insist on the need to explore the ways in which a specific biographical pathology—itself necessarily a historical phenomenon and a social fact, by virtue of its very existence as an unconscious symptom—constitutes under certain circumstances a recording apparatus for a unique historical content that it can alone disclose and bring to objective expression. The grotesque depersonalization demanded by this Utopia in order to come into being is then enabled, as in some ruse of history, by Platonov's own peculiar temperament, which can thus be seen as historically necessary, however much a biographical accident it may also have been.

But to put things this way is also necessarily to recall the peasant background of this Utopia, and the way in which it is determined by the equally contingent intersection between a peasant way of life and a peasant mentality everywhere in the process of liquidation today and an essentially modernist project of social revolution (along with an essentially modernist formal structure in this narrative). This structural peculiarity demands to be juxtaposed with whatever psychoanalytic structures are posited on the basis of Platonov's peculiar style and his narrative production.

Our own relationship to this text can, to be sure, be rehearsed in many different ways, only a few of which have found expression in the preceding pages: the postmodernities have themselves much to learn from this archaic specimen of modernism, fresh as though out of a time capsule, owing to its recent discovery as well as to the historic omission of any specifically modernist moment from Soviet history, an anachronistic survival with its hair and fingernails still growing as it were. Postmodern and poststructural conceptions of the dissociation of the subject and the extinction of its centeredness are in particular challenged by the conception of the "eunuch of the soul," which somehow exhibits this familiar postmodern motif of the death of the subject from a starkly unfamiliar or defamiliarized and properly modernist standpoint.

Meanwhile, the sacrality of the high modern text—if not its religious dimension then at least its more Heideggerian vocation to serve as the vehicle for the deconcealing of truth—here seems to reach an outer edge, where it suggests affinities with some of the great nontheological visions such as Buddhism. Here too, however, it seems best to defer such lessons for a more formal examination of the implications between the Utopian text and such metaphysical or postmetaphysical content. For the relationship between Utopia and death is an essential one, but not because of any mystical properties of death itself: rather, death is the aftereffect and the sign that the perspective of Utopia has been reached, which consists in a great and progressive distance from all individual and existential experience, from individual people, from *characters* (to raise the related issue of Utopian discourse versus narrative or storytelling). The emergence of death is then at that point the signal that it has been possible to take the point of view of the species upon human existence. Utopia necessarily takes the point of view of the species upon human history, thus emptying it of much that we consider not merely historical but irreplaceably significant in human life. For the urgent specificity of historical events is at one with their uniqueness and their contingency: the irrevocable moment when this special possibility had to be grasped or forever lost. History is the most intense experience of this unique fusion of time and the event, temporality and action; history is choice, freedom, and failure all at once, inevitable failure, but not death. Utopia is set at a height from which those changes are no longer visible: even if the Utopia in question is one of absolute change, change is nonetheless viewed from that well-nigh glacial and inhuman standpoint as absolute repetition, as a sameness of change as far as the eye can reach. A state of society that does not need history or historical struggle lies beyond much that is precious to us in individual as well as collective existence; its thought obliges us to confront the most terrifying dimension of our humanity, at least for the individualism of modern, bourgeois people, and that is our species being, our insertion in the great chain of the generations, which we know as death. Utopia is inseparable from death in that its serenity gazes calmly and implacably away from the accidents of individual existence and the inevitability of its giving way: in this sense it might even be said that Utopia solves the problem of death, by inventing a new way of looking at individual death, as a matter of limited concern, beyond all stoicism.

Utopia is also many other things and brings other requirements with it; but it is this as well, so that it may not be so great a paradox to find Utopian lessons, which is to say a hint and a beginning of Utopian representation, in Kafka's grim story *Josephina the Singer; or, the Mice People.* Not really a story exactly or a narrative (and in that very much like Utopian discourse), this text would seem to be a parable of the artist rather than a blueprint for communal living; even though the alternate title underscores a Gestalt alternation whereby these pages—which have but two "characters" in any traditional sense, Josephina and "the people,"—can be read fully as much as a presentation of the latter as they are a dramatization of the former, who in that case becomes the representational pretext that alone makes the collective subject fitfully visible.

Kafka, the most logical of writers since the great alternating periodic sentences of the eighteenth century, not only shifts with monotonous regularity between the twin subjects of his double title, but also between the *pour* and the *contre*, between an affirmation and a negation equally predictable in their alternation, whose implacable rhythm—"but," "yet," "doch"— makes up the fateful neutrality of his style. In this tale, however, the alternating rhythm is itself a philosophical concept or category, and expresses the unresolvable paradoxes of art and culture, in fully as analytic a fashion as Marcuse was to do a few years later in his great essay, "The Affirmative Character of Culture." For art is the faithful expression of society—and thus the *same* as it—at the same time that as a representation of society and its self-consciousness it must also be *different* from its object. *Josephina* is, then, one sustained extraordinary exercise in the passage back and forth between this identity and this difference.

Thus: Josephina's music is great, but we are not a musical people. Yet perhaps Josephina's "music" is not musical either, but is rather constituted by "*pfeifen,*" "piping," which in fact all of us do. Is she therefore supremely different from all of us, or exactly the same as all of us? The former, surely, because even in her very ordinary piping, she frames the performance and makes of it a ritual; thus, "we admire in her what we do not at all admire in ourselves" (195/130),* which is to say

---

*Page references in the text are first to the German text, *Samtliche Erzählungen,* ed. Paul Raabe (Frankfurt: Fischer, 1973), and then to the English translation by Willa and Edwin Muir, in *The Basic Kafka,* ed. Erich Heller (New York: Pocket Books, 1979).

that despite her deliberate performance, she is not different but the same. Yet we are silent and she sings.

Meanwhile, her vocation is stimulated by the great crises (even though, for the people of the mice, every day is a crisis, fraught with extreme danger). But by assembling us she often puts us in crisis and in extreme danger, making us vulnerable to our mortal enemies (203/139).

She taxes her own forces and her body to the utmost, imagining that in such crises she is protecting us (199/134); whereas in fact her hold over us is that we imagine ourselves to be protecting her, as pitiful and vulnerable as she seems to us (199/133). Nor does this moment bear only on the role the charismatic artist plays for her public: one thinks also of guerrilla warfare, and of Frances FitzGerald's account of the anti-Confucianism of the Vietcong, whose astute strategy lay in assuring the people of the villages, We are not your father; you are our mother. At this point, then, the theme of the tale shifts from art (difference) to collectivity (identity), with this proviso that only the intervention of art and the theme of the great artist could make it possible to grasp the essential anonymity of the people, who have no feeling for art, no reverence for the artist, no place for the aesthetic: so that, as we shall see, these enabling representational pretexts must at a final limit again cancel themselves out.

So it is that Josephina lets the people be what they already are: uniquely, she causes them to assemble in silence—would this be possible without her ("how can our gatherings take place in utter silence?" [209/145])? She constitutes the necessary element of exteriority that alone permits immanence to come into being: "we too are soon sunk in the feeling of the mass, that, warmly pressed body to body, listens with indrawn breath" (197/132); "as if the harried individual once in a while could relax and stretch himself at ease in the great, warm bed of the community" (203/138). Her performance is in reality "not so much a performance of songs as an assembly of the people" (200/135); and Kafka's story thus ultimately derives from the same mysteries from which political philosophy itself emerges, from the riddle of Rousseau's general will, and of the paradoxes of collective representation. For Josephina's art "comes almost like a message from the whole people to each individual; Josephina's thin piping amidst grave decisions is almost like our people's precarious existence amidst the tumult of a hostile world" (200/136). She is thus the vehicle for the collectivity's affirmation of itself: she reflects their collective identity back to them. But at one and the same time, she then immediately demands special privileges (exemption from physical labor) as a compensation for her labor or indeed as a recognition of her unique distinction and her irreplaceable service to the community.

It is perhaps the high point of Kafka's tale, and nowhere is the icy indifference of this Utopia of democracy more astonishingly revealed (but revealed by way of nothing and no reaction) than in the refusal of the people to grant her this form of individual difference: "the people listen to her arguments and pay no attention" (204/140).

> Suppose that instead of the people one had an individual to deal with: one might imagine that this man had been giving in to Josephina all the time while nursing a wild desire to put an end to his submissiveness one fine day; that he had made superhuman sacrifices for Josephina in the firm belief that there was a natural limit to his capacity for sacrifice; yes, that he had sacrificed more than was needful merely to hasten the process, merely to spoil Josephina and encourage her to ask for more and more until she did indeed reach the limit with this last petition of hers; and that he then cut her off with a final refusal which was curt because long held in reserve.   (205–6/141–142)

But the people is precisely not an individual or a character in this sense, nor are Kafka's logical alternatives of positive and negative sequential and diachronic, like a story of action and

reaction, in which the one might be explained as a compensation for the other. Rather they are synchronic and simultaneous: the essence of the people lies in this absolute indifference
to individuals. Insofar as Josephina causes the essence of the
people to appear, she also causes this essential indifference
of the anonymous and the radically democratic equally to
emerge. Her difference, by revealing identity, is then canceled
by the force of that absolute collective identity.

It is thus no longer certain that she is a great artist in the
first place (indeed, it is possible that "the mere fact of our
listening to her is proof that she is no singer" [201/136]); she
is in fact pathetic and ludicrous (although we never laugh at
her [198/133]), and her pretensions are childish. But our
children have no childhood; and the aesthetic of play Josephina
represents (difference) can have no equivalent in our lives.
Her art is thus supremely ambiguous: "something of our poor
brief childhood is in it, something of lost happiness that can
never be found again [difference, a reality of art utterly opposed to the conditions of life] but also something of active
daily life, of its small gaieties, unaccountable and yet springing
up and not to be obliterated [identity, art reflecting the conditions of the social] (203/139)."

The sounding of the theme of childhood is therefore at one
with the sounding of the theme of death, and of generations:
children have no childhood, but "the fertility of our race"
causes "one generation to tread on the heels of another, the
children have no time to be children"; children thus dramatize
not merely the fleeting sequence of generations but somehow
absolute difference as well, they are children who have no
time to be children—they have a merely negative existence as
what prevents the previous generation from knowing childhood in the first place:

> And not the same children, as in those schools, no, always
> new children again and again, without end, without a
> break, hardly does a child appear than it is no more a child,

while behind it new childish faces are already crowding so
fast and so thick they are indistinguishable.   (201/137)

But this means not merely death in general and collectively
but also the death of Josephina in particular: what can remain
of her if she is unique? And here the story turns against itself,
and having made reflections of a general and nonnarrative
nature, which are presumably always the case, now shifts gears
into the temporal ("that happened a day or two ago"), at which
point the very paradox of the historical existence of Josephina
is underscored, as well as the absolute tension that obtains
between the Utopia of the absolute community and the history
of the unique and of the event. Josephina will presumably then
become history, as they say—only we have no history and
detest historians. Her unique historical glory will thus be to be
forgotten: Josephina "will happily lose herself in the number-
less throng of the heroes of our people, and soon, since we
are no historians, will rise to the heights of redemption and be
forgotten like all her brothers" (209/145). Difference is effaced by the identity it was alone able to reveal for an instant.
Utopia is precisely the elevation from which this species forgetfulness and oblivion—quite the opposite of what obtains
for animals who have no individuation to begin with—takes
place; it is anonymity as an intensely positive force, as the
most fundamental fact of life of the democratic community;
and it is this anonymity that in our non- or pre-Utopian world
goes under the name and characterization of death. It seems
appropriate to use *Chevengur* as a source for such Utopian
reeducation, as we have here used Kafka.

The Constraints of Postmodernism

PART THREE

As I suggested in my introduction, the organizing frame of this section is, if not structural, then at least typological: the very framework itself is an argument, and was designed to show that the rich plurality of styles that postmodernism often enough celebrates about itself can be sorted out into tendencies that form a system. A system in this sense is at one and the same time freedom and determination: it opens a set of creative possibilities (which are alone possible as responses to the situation it articulates) as well as tracing ultimate limits of praxis that are also the limits of thought and imaginative projection. So if it is true it lies, and we would have no way of knowing we were locked into it, no way of drawing the boundary lines in which we are ourselves contained. By the same token, such a scheme wants to be objective but can never be anything more than ideological: for it becomes very difficult indeed to think how we might distinguish the real existence of the various kinds into which modern building falls from the patent invention of various systems of those kinds in our own heads. There is, in fact, something of a false problem here: the nagging worry, about whether we are in fact drawing our own eye, can be assuaged to a certain degree by the reminder that our eye is itself part of the very system of Being that is our object of speculation. Better to have drawn our eye—as a local fragment of that immense system of Being—than to find the last feeble light source in the cave extinguished altogether! In fact, then, the productive systems of the artists and architects come from the same place as the thinking about the features that might somehow define and describe them: it is all of a piece, all postmodern somehow, by virtue of that Zeitgeist whose existence is presupposed here, if not conjectured.

At that point of indistinction, then, when the diagnosis is also its own symptom, can one continue to speak of argument, let alone of proof (not to think of falsifiability)? A certain conviction that you are working in the right direction comes, I think, when the traits or semes of the semiotic square begin to accumulate interesting synonyms from different systems: thus "replication" begins to resonate with the vibrations of "intertextuality," while the kinship between formal innovation (in the high modern) and the theoretical vanguardism of a much later period is reinforced. These overlaps are in reality something like arguments in their own right, implied theories of local history waiting to be exfoliated. The moment in which a seme from one kind of movement begins to coincide with that of another is a kind of discovery procedure, which, far from reconfirming what we know (or think we know) already—surely the basic fear about a thought suspected of being little more than a projection of itself onto the outside world—leads to new interpretations.

By the same token, falsifiability is here simply the unfurling of a list of features, traits, and semes that can find no place at all in the current system, even though they exist and demand attention. It might be said that rather than disproving the scheme, this mode of objection simply renders it trivial. If, on the other hand, a different scheme—with its own simultaneous contraries and contradictories—is proposed, then what results is a quarrel of interpretations that far from putting an end to one of its starting points, is more likely to lead on into something similar, but unimaginably more complex: an outcome that, on my view, would tend to confirm the fruitfulness of the current hypothesis, in however perverse and backhanded a fashion.

Contrary to what Hegel thought and tried to put into practice, with the semiotic square—owing to its synchronic nature—the story of the origins of this or that feature can do little to illuminate the dynamics of the thing itself: there is therefore always a difficulty in beginning in any nondogmatic way, and that problem will here be avoided by following the very logic of the term itself and proposing that it is clearly enough modernism that is the situation of postmodernism and the starting point for any number of the latter's developments. These then prove, on closer inspection, to be simple inversions, negations, and cancelations of features normally attributed to modernism. The unintended consequence of this procedure would be the conclusion that postmodernism is little more than modernism after all (or that it is parasitic or belated with respect to the latter's achievements). I am very far from wanting to endorse that kind of view, but it might be sidestepped by adopting the hypothesis that, at least at its beginnings, the negation, inversion, or cancellation of high modernism was what the first postmoderns thought they were up to, while in the process of generating something altogether different.

This seems at least to be the case with the twin semes into which we begin by articulating high modernism here: both are scandals for current postmodern doxa, so that we may well be allowed to begin by positing the fundamental features or semes of high modernism in a kind of demiurgic impulse in which a desire called totality is somehow, impossibly, conjoined with a desire called innovation or simply the New. The question will inevitably arise, however, why these two things should be thought of as an opposition, as standing in a contradictory tension with one another. That is a very interesting question, which would lead on into the scholastics of the modern itself; I here assume that it is the constitution of an immense monadic style, that phenomenological world which is the form and appearance the category of totality takes in all the great modern artists from the literature of Proust and Joyce to the architecture of Frank Lloyd Wright and Mies, from Wagner's *Gesamtkunstwerk* or Schoenberg's post-tonal system to the very different painterly totalities of Kandinsky's or Malevich's mystical systems and of Picasso's protean multiplicities. If so, it is precisely these immense monadic efforts—enormous, unthinkable synchronicities—that divert attention from the diachronic originalities of the artists in question as they punctually tinker with this or that technique or feature of their immediate predecessor (in such a way that the tinkering, the minute local revision generates a whole illusion of new work, in a kind of vast aesthetic "motivation of the device" in the familiar expression of the Russian Formalists). The two perspectives are perhaps merely optional ones: still, they open up lines of flight that put a rather different spin on the works in question, now immense, self-sufficient, timeless substances à la Spinoza, now moments in a patient diachronic chain, in the telos of the modern as it cancels what went before and patiently invents a new Novum for the new present.

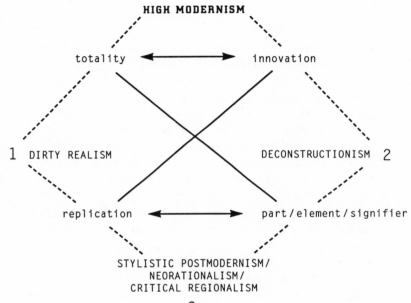

HIGH MODERNISM

totality ⟷ innovation

1 DIRTY REALISM DECONSTRUCTIONISM 2

replication ⟷ part / element / signifier

STYLISTIC POSTMODERNISM/
NEORATIONALISM/
CRITICAL REGIONALISM

3

I

At any rate this starting point now raises interesting questions about the status of both these categories, Totality and Innovation, in the era of the postmodern. As far as the first of these is concerned, at least, it seems appropriate to interrogate the category of Totality in the light of that contemporary (or postcontemporary) architect whose work most dramatically and unexpectedly returns to the project of larger form and of large buildings. Rem Koolhaas has indeed characterized his own initial (theoretical) interest in the United States (in his remarkable book *Delirious New York*) as a kind of intellectual sublimation of the vocation for large scale that he was unable to realize practically in the narrower confines of the European nation-states and in particular of his native Holland. European integration then opened up this situation unexpectedly, and made the large project into a practical possibility. Koolhaas has himself enthusiastically embraced this possibility, above all in the grand designs for the Library of France ("la très grande bibliothèque") in Paris and for the Sea Trade Center in Zeebrugge, Belgium, the entry point into Europe of the ferry lines that will henceforth have to compete with the "Chunnel." (One might also include, among such projects, the Art and Media Center in Karlsruhe and the Congrexpo in Lille, as well as the Convention Center in Agadir, but not, perhaps, the individual dwellings and apartment buildings, which—no less formally interesting—would rather seem to embody the lyric side of what is otherwise an epic impulse.)

The relevance of such projects for us is that both in their very different ways give body to a will to include an entire world within themselves: one of information and the various traditions of signs, in the library, the other the multitudinous consequences of the media in its other major acceptation, namely as transport and physical conveyance. Unlike the modern project, these public ventures must underscore the exclusion of private life, and they necessarily reincorporate the paradoxes of private property after the end of civil society (in the one, by way of the dialectic of the property of information; in the other, by way of the more classic antinomy of a public space that is privately owned).

What is of interest for us in the present context is the metamorphosis these new projects inflect upon the older modernist categories of envelopment, incorporation, containership, and finally the duality of inside and outside that all the older forms implied in one way or another. The enormous box that houses the Library of France, for example, rebukes traditional conceptions of the shell or the shape by its very enormity, attempting, as I will argue in a moment, by the prosaic nature of the form to escape formal perception altogether. What this nonform specifically negates, I believe, is the grandest of modernist, Corbusean conceptions of the essentially expressive relationship between the interior and its outer plastic lines and walls, which were to shed their rigidity and simply follow their functions in such a way as to correspond aesthetically to the rather different realities within. This was then a kind of hermeneutic aesthetic, by virtue of which the existential and spatial properties of the various forms of activity within (the former rooms, here abolished by the free plan) were as it were transferred to the rather different materials of the outside surfaces, with their properties of visualization and photographability. The expressive correspondence (one would want to strengthen this into a well-nigh Althusserian diagnostic concept on the order and with the rigor of his well-known "expressive causality") is virtually a preallegorical or symbolic one; it is a kind of one-to-one matching in which the problem of representation itself (or translation) seems to disappear, leaving us with the freshness of a kind of new nature in these non- and postnatural clean Corbusean forms, of which Venturi has said that they are to be assimilated to sculptures rather than to buildings (or perhaps to buildings so ashamed of

that condition that they long to disguise themselves as sculptures).

The new concept that Koolhaas's large scale now produces may be formulated rather in terms of *incommensurability*. Here the functions, the rooms, the interior, the inner spaces, hang within their enormous container like so many floating organs. The model indeed shows them up as though endowed with a kind of X-ray existence within the immense, now virtually translucent cube. Koolhaas has himself indeed invented a remarkable figure in order to characterize this unusual, untraditional mode of being within: "In this block," he says, "the major public spaces are defined as absences of building, voids carved out from the information solid. Floating in memory, they are like multiple embryos, each with their own technological placenta" (*El Croquis,* 68). Meanwhile, the contents of the various large-scale projects can also be seen as a selection of all the geometric forms and solids imaginable: an enormous random collection of solids, cones, cubes, pyramids, spheres,

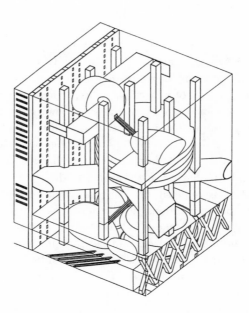

and so on, such that what they are housed or collected in (as it were the notorious "class of all classes") does not itself fall under any of those geometrical types or categories and must be dismissively referred to as a "block." Something about the essence of a model or maquette as such seems at stake here, and auto-referred, in distinction to "paper architecture," to the usual stereometric drawing, let alone the glossy photographic plate or colored image; it is as though these projects also somehow attempted to realize the Platonic ideal of the "model" as such.

Formally, what the emergence of this new category of "floating organs" does is to problematize and ultimately to dispel any last illusion of the possibility of a Corbusean expressive correspondence. This does not, however, undermine the category of translation itself but rather, in the form of transcoding, intensifies it to a new conceptual luminscence. For just as the inner shapes and organs coexist, tranquilly missing each other in space or interpenetrating without touching each other—in the same way that the activities with which they are associated convey so many dimensions that overlap without coinciding—reading with eating, for example, or the consumption of images with the participation in conferences—so also in this very spatial simultaneity the notion of the incommensurable waxes, and along with it the urge and will to translate the givens of any single dimension into another one: an impulse which, impossible of realization, evolves all the more, battening on its very frustration, into the sheer concept of transcoding itself. This goes well beyond anything organic in the conventional ideological sense (of a complete body, of organic wholeness and harmony); it even presses the modernist notion of the organic beyond its limits (as when Joyce underscored the radical functional difference of each organ by assigning it to the radically different stylistic dynamics of each of his virtually autonomous chapters). Presupposed here is that ultimate rejoining and reidentification of the organic with the mechanical that Deleuze and Donna Haraway, each in his or her very different ways, theorize and celebrate; but within a category—that of totality—alien to either of them.

Meanwhile, the Zeebrugge Terminal, like the helmet of an immense cosmonaut, part plastic part metal, "a cross between a ball and a cone" (*El Croquis,* 80), includes, in the same nonspecifiable way, whole former structures, such as a hotel and an office building, along with the *rose des sables* of the on- and off-ramps, as delicately interlaced as the great Figueroa grade crossing in downtown Los Angeles: allegories, perhaps, of that other intestinal necessity of the modern building about which Koolhaas has frequently complained, that of the pipes and wiring, the "services" ("it is unbelievable how a component that amounts to one third of the section of a building and may represent 50 percent of the budget is in a way inaccessible to architectural thought" [13]), whose problematic he elsewhere

dramatized, as an opportunity rather than a dilemma, in his "theory" of the elevator (discussed in Part One), where the existence of such a central mechanism seemed to offer a way of concentrating everything heterogeneous and external together in a governable fashion.

Yet the necessary existence of internal multiplicity persists, a reality for which the word *heterogeneity* is too weak, at least in part precisely because multiplicity is here included and somehow contained and implies a whole new conception of the relationship between individual items, formerly always figures on a ground, or ensembles artfully and harmoniously combined and constructed. Here, however, floating means a radical absence of ground as such, let alone the end of even more traditional conceptions of perspective, imbrication, artful contrast, arrangement, and the like. But this now begins to produce a new category of its own, of which we must still imperfectly speak in terms of part or element or compo-

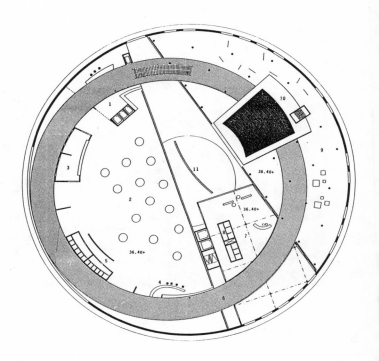

OFFICE FOR METROPOLITAN ARCHITECTURE
BOOMPJES 55, ROTTERDAM 2011XB   FAX. 010 - 411 41 95   TEL. 010 - 411 12 16

SEA TERMINAL 'ZEEBRUGGE',

LOBBY

BLAD 8

1 LOBBY HOTEL   2 RESTAURANT   3 KEUKEN   4 BAR   5 TOILETTEN   6 RONDGANG   7 KANTOREN   8 TOILETTEN
9 EXPOSITIE/PROMOTIEVLAK   10 CINEMA   11 FILM/VIDEO SCREEN

nent, and that now in its turn begins to generate a semiotic position in its own right, something like the absolute contradictory of the category of totality, which, as we shall see shortly, defines a rather different situation and a rather different set of formal problems for other postmodern or postcontemporary architects.

For the moment, however, we must turn our attention to a different angle of the semiotic square: for the Koolhaas we have so far evoked, if his work is characterized only in terms of the desire called totality, risks being assimilated back into the modernist paradigm itself (for which, to be sure, he himself admits some small nostalgia). To anticipate, we will call the other operative feature of his work—a resolutely non- or antimodern one—the engagement with the issue and problem of *replication* as such—that is to say, the obligation to come to terms with the city fabric and the cultural patterning into which the building, even that on so large a scale, is thrust. But for Koolhaas, as indeed for other consequent modern artists, this issue of the fabric is in reality at one with that of large scale, an expression that can designate both the individual building and also the urban in general. If modern architecture is in general characterized by the dilemma of a radical split between the architectural and the urban, the concept of replication can be read as a novel way of addressing that gap, not by synthesis or reconstruction but by way of reduplication (or even of *scaling,* to use Peter Eisenman's concept).

But this solution is what emerged from one of the classic texts of contemporary theory, *Learning from Las Vegas,* by Venturi, Scott-Brown, and Izenour (a work that it would be misguided to classify as an exclusively architectural study; it could also be read as a manifesto for the newly emerging "cultural studies"). *Learning from Las Vegas* starts from the premise that architectural high modernism viewed the modern industrial city as a pathology that it was the task of great architecture to overcome; the great modern building was to begin to do this by way of a radical act of separation and disjunction from that diseased city fabric: the insalubrious, reeking, airless, sodden alleys of a dead inherited medieval city, the industrial slums of a modern agglomeration—best to do away with those streets altogether, to open all that to sun and fresh air by an act of joyous destruction, and to erect, in places once weighed down by the most impenetrable *Mietkaserne* and cobblestones, exhilarating high-rises rearing off their ground on *pilotis* that stood as a symbol of defiance and refusal of, escape from, the old world, the old Europe, the nineteenth century.

But looking back from the 1960s in the United States, all this modernized excitement, akin to the thrill of the radio and the transatlantic ocean liner (lit up like a city at sea), palls into the sheerest upper-class elitism—repugnance for the illiteracy of immigrants, and for their enforced lack of hygiene, and lack of taste or respect. The aesthetic attitude thus seems to shed its skin and reveal the social and political face of an ivy-league aristocracy we no longer acknowledge. *Learning from Las Vegas,* indeed, explicitly proposes the linguistic version of the matter. The "fallen" city fabric ("who would have thought death had undone so many?") is in reality a vernacular, even more than a mélange of accents and ungrammatical expressions of ignorance; it can be spoken and learned in its own right, and indeed the urban architect ought to speak that and not invent a high modern idiolect of his own choosing on the grounds that it is purer and less alienated (this kind of alienation theory now coming to seem the conservative cultural pathos of the old elites).

These excellent sentiments, which would seem to urge us in the direction of a vernacular architecture (where it is difficult to separate out the national-American from the secular-modernized), then begin to raise new problems of their own. The city fabric is now to be endorsed, rather than reformed or replaced, but the status of the individual building within that fabric, even if it now "speaks the same language," is less clear:

who needs architects at all if it is simply to be a question of putting up more of the same (a process presumably not in any danger of being interrupted, at least not in the American city)? Venturi's answer retains one of the central categories of the high modern, namely Irony; it proposes that the new, architect-designed building stand out ever so slightly from the vernacular surrounding it by way of a barely perceptible ironic distance, the merest thickening and distillation of a self-consciousness in the speaking, like the faintest quotation marks around a familiar colloquial outburst. One takes the point; but it does not quite seem to work, particularly since irony itself was traditionally a sign fully as much as a weapon of just those condescending upper classes from which we were supposed to escape.

A rather different answer seems possible, which now returns us to that category of totality from which, as an emblem of the high-modernist enemy, we had thought we were emerging, advancing from the "monumental duck," the modernist sculpture symbolic of a whole Rilkean "change of life," out into the miracle mile and the freeways of the vernacular developments as they devour ever more of the surrounding former countryside. For a moment (which now seems past), this new "fabric" was also described in terms of chaos theory: not a vernacular you learned to speak (like black English) but the outer edge of the way the neo-universe lawfully produces, not homogeneity and standardization but a genuine postmodern heterogeneity (consistent with the freedom of the market itself). Now the new individual building does not even have a fabric into which to "fit," like some well-chosen word; it no longer has the option of constituting some part of speech of a vernacular linguistic production, rather it must somehow merely *replicate* the chaos and the turbulences all around it. But under these circumstances the individual construction can once again discover a vocation to enact the totality, albeit in an inversion of the modernist gesture. As in Hegel's inverted world, Le Corbusier wanted to conjure into being a micro-cosm that was the opposite of the fallen real conditions and their Utopian transformation; what will shortly be referred to as "dirty realism" can now aspire to offering a microcosm that replicates those conditions and within its new type of closure simulates all the chaotic libidinal freedom of the now danger-ous world outside. It is the passage from the amusement park to the mall: now private police and concealed cameras sanitize the unruliness of the older collective experience and make it accessible to aesthetic and postmodern reception. Replication meanwhile also means the depoliticization of the former mod-ern, the consent to corporate power and its grants and con-tracts, the reduction of social conscience to manageable, prac-tical, pragmatic limits; the Utopian becomes unmentionable, along with socialism and unbalanced budgets. Clearly also, on any materialist view, the way the building forms fall out is of enormous significance; in particular the proportion of individ-ual houses to office buildings, the possibility or not of urban ensembles, the rate of commissions for public buildings such as opera houses or museums (often recontained within those reservation spaces of private or public universities, which are among the most signal sources of high-class contemporary patronage), and not least the chance to design apartment buildings or public housing. (I have argued elsewhere that the private home rebuilt by Frank Gehry, one of the most remark-able achievements of postcontemporary architecture, is fully as much to be considered an exemplification of such "dirty real-ism" as are the grandiose new totalities of Koolhaas with which we have been concerned.)

We will see shortly how these works, which on our scheme preserve a certain, narrowly specifiable share of the modernist impulse as such, are to be distinguished from those other, more characteristic postmodernisms that more completely re-pudiate that impulse, while exploring the possibilities of repli-cation in rather different ways from this.

Before doing so, however, we must now retrace our steps, and in a long digression explain the peculiar title that has been selected for the quadrant just examined, and for the work of Rem Koolhaas in particular.

Dirty realism is a suggestive term applied to architecture by Liane Lefaivre that deserves further meditation and speculation. She herself found the term in an essay by Bill Buford in *Granta* on recent U.S. writing, in particular on the new American short story; it may be worth quoting Buford's own remarks about this new trend he feels himself able to identify and to distinguish from Mailer-type existentialism or new-novel-type poststructural fabulation or indeed other kinds of writing that make "the large historical statement."

> It is instead a fiction of a different scope—devoted to the local details, the nuances, the little disturbances in language and gesture—and it is entirely appropriate that its primary form is the short story and that it is so conspicuously part of the American short story revival. But these are strange stories: unadorned, unfurnished, low-rent tragedies about people who watch day-time television, read cheap romances or listen to country and western music. They are waitresses in roadside cafés, cashiers in supermarkets, construction workers, secretaries and unemployed cowboys. They play bingo, eat cheeseburgers, hunt deer and stay in cheap hotels. They drink a lot and are often in trouble: for stealing a car, breaking a window, pickpocketing a wallet. They are from Kentucky or Alabama or Oregon, but, mainly, they could just about be from anywhere: drifters in a world cluttered with junk food and the oppressive details of modern consumerism.   ("Introduction" 4)

Lefaivre, however, tries out this interesting new slogan on Gehry and Koolhaas—which already opens up a breach in the concept, or so it seems to me. She refers—quite rightly in my opinion—to *Blade Runner,* whereby the breach is significantly enlarged; and if you added that new kind of science-fictional production called "cyberpunk," it would be enlarged even more dramatically, indeed, virtually beyond repair. But how can a term or slogan, about which we do not even yet know what its object is, stage itself as inappropriate and begin to modify its own meaning and to correct itself, as it were in the linguistic void, before the emergence of any reality with which it can be compared?

This is, I think, because the slogan carries its breach within itself and is so far merely acting out the internal dynamic of its own structure, which is not merely twofold (the question of how "realism" could be or get "dirty") but tripartite insofar as the declared intent to apply a term such as *realism* to architecture in the first place raises problems of its own and incites to conjecture. If by realism we mean mimesis of some sort, then it is certainly not clear from the outset how any architecture could be considered realistic: Le Corbusier's white walls, the ascetic absence of ornament, the Bauhaus's functionalisms, can surely not be considered any more realistic in any of the possible senses than the Gothic revival or neoclassicism or the wildest fantasies of Gaudi.

A mimesis derived from the Venturi-Rauch-Brown replication, or "speaking the vernacular," seems to offer a more promising line on architectural "realism," dirty or not; but before we adopt it let's look again at the spatial features of Buford's description: "day-time television" is evoked, along with "roadside cafes," "supermarkets," and "cheap hotels" (why not motels, one wonders), there is petty crime and junk food and "modern consumerism." These are familiar features of daily life in the superstate from which, it should be noted, high modernism in the United States—in theory and in practice alike, fifties aestheticism organized around Pound and Henry James and Wallace Stevens and the New Criticism—

was in desperate flight; of our great modern writers, only Nabokov handled this kind of material, in *Lolita,* which thereby at once became The Great American Novel,—but of course he was a foreigner to begin with. The transformation of these daily-life materials is I believe a dual process: on the one hand, it seems to have involved a prodigious enlargement of what we call culture, by way of the media and the informatization of daily life. Here narrative raw materials, which (in an earlier "realist" moment) could still look non- or precultural, now slowly seem to undergo the process of a transformation into images and simulacra. Meanwhile, in some other loop of this momentous historical shift, a high literature or a literary and cultural modernism, whose essential specificity and definition turned on its radical separation from the daily life and the kitsch cultural consumption of the great middle-class public, itself becomes slowly effaced (in what we now call the post-modern).

Here the distinction between high and low art begins to fade and the elegance of high technological media production to vie with older conceptions of artistic value; but this process coexists with another one, in which the older distinctions between city and country, metropolis and provinces, cease to be operative, and in which the United States becomes standardized from one coast to the other and all along its new superhighway system, everything in American life thereby falling into commodification. The imagification or culturalization of daily life thus accompanies and is virtually indistinguishable from the gradual identification of mass culture with Culture itself, the end of modernism or the canon, the arrival of pop, and later on of the postmodern, in short: the harnessing of modern elite cultural forms of all kinds to big business and corporate production for mass consumption.

So the new literature Buford speaks of is one that follows and reflects this transformation of everyday life by the penetration of a corporate mass culture into its utmost recesses and crannies, with the consequent colonization and elimination of any of the residual enclaves that had hitherto remained exempt; those were enclaves of farming life just as fully as spaces of high culture, they were ghetto or community spaces fully as much as traditional village or classical urban forms of collective living.

The problem with Buford's description is then what orients it toward those particular short-story writers he wants to specify, to differentiate, and to celebrate as a new and distinctive cultural tendency in late capitalism. The characters of such stories, he tells us, as though in passing, "are from Kentucky or Alabama or Oregon, but, mainly, they could just about be from anywhere." But there's the rub, and this rub will turn out to be of the greatest interest for us: they cannot be from just about anywhere, Buford has here named nonurban areas. In fact, his writers are what have come to be called neoregionalist writers, and it will be this that opens the rift between his slogan and the literary objects to which he wants to apply it. (Indeed, our own typological scheme reflects this objection strongly and deeply in the way in which it seeks sharply to distinguish between dirty realism and critical regionalism, whatever those two things may turn out to be.)

Neoregionalism, like the neo-ethnic, is a specifically postmodern form of reterritorialization; it is a flight from the realities of late capitalism, a compensatory ideology, in a situation in which regions (like ethnic groups) have been fundamentally wiped out—reduced, standardized, commodified, atomized, or rationalized. The ideology of regionalism is the sentimentalization, by the short-story writers in question, of the nature of the social life and the socioeconomic system in the superstate today. It seeks, by including the detritus of junk-food wrappers and the broken windows of vandalized cars, to validate its credentials as a realistic representation of North American life which can in the process reassure North Americans as to the persistence of a distinctive regional or urban social life about which everything else in our experience testifies that it has already long since disappeared. Buford's neoregional writers then perform another crucial ideological move, duly registered in his own perceptive critical apparatus, and that is to certify the microscopic and the inconsequential—or rather what the state and the dominant institutions pronounce to be trivial and insignificant—as the space of real life, or of what used to be authentic. Indeed, it is because hegemonic thought and institutional value is thus understood as valorizing what in the previous paragraph Buford characterizes as "the large historical statement" (what is "heroic or grand," and seems to involve "epic ambitions" that now "seem in contrast inflated, strange or even false"—he mentions Mailer and Bellow, Gaddis and Pynchon)—it is because such large or megastatements are thought to be institutionalized and hegemonic, and to wear the stamp of approval of the State that the new microfiction can be packaged as protest, revolt, subversion, and the like.

On the other hand, anyone familiar with current ideological debates can recognize a somewhat different one, as it profiles itself behind this respectably anarchist position; and that is the well-known "war on totality" under whose banner a postmodern anti-Marxism pursues targets that it claims to identify with state power (if not with the economic system) but that are in reality the now disorganized forces of a repudiation of late capitalism and of a Utopian intent to continue to imagine radical alternatives. In terms of this polemic, then, what here gives itself off as the minute and the local is in reality the strategic new value of the fragment and the nontotalizable, the ephemeral constellation, the fuzzy set, the disposable, provisional, and fictive scale model. I think it is important to fight this particular battle out (a battle based, in my opinion, on a misunderstanding of what the concept of totality and the act of totalization really are), but I have raised the issue here mainly in order to show the entanglement, within Buford's statement or program, of several distinct and only distantly related ideologemes, which, disentangled, give a rather different picture. The matter of the local and of totality will of course remain in our larger typology as obligatory semes or features; the pull of the regional is here clearly registered and will certainly be acknowledged in our final scheme; but I will now argue that a somewhat different conception of dirty realism must be advanced, which is in fact much closer to Liane Lefaivre's architectural version than to the Buford statement with which she herself began.

For the fateful gesture in her description, which in my opinion necessarily displaces Buford's short-story writers to some very different (and more regional or neoregional) zone of modern reality and culture, is the mention of the film *Blade Runner,* which, with its literary analogy called "cyberpunk," has touched a nerve, struck a chord, sounded a note, of crucial symptomatic importance in the postcontemporary political unconscious, in that ideological objective spirit in which we store up our social imaginary and accumulate various fantasy pictures (of no little active reality) of the global system we blindly inhabit. Cyberpunk indeed seems to me a more promising starting point than Buford's localist and suburban fiction for the pursuit of a definition of dirty realism, not least because it is urban, and also because its nightmares are also on the point of becoming celebrations of a new reality, a new reality-intensification, that cannot simply be dealt with by a reactivation of the older cultural and class attitudes.

I want to discuss cyberpunk under two headings—as a sequel to naturalism, and as a symptomal representation of the end of civil society—before returning to its architectural expression in the newer works of Rem Koolhaas.

Naturalism offers a useful comparison here since it was if anything the original "dirty realism," what the French call a *"misérabilisme"* in which the lower depths, the forbidden spaces of the new industrial city, were disclosed to a horrified bourgeois readership in the form of perilous journeys and accounts of the pathetic destinies of the various underclasses, which you could read about in your comfortable armchair, and that thereby offered the double bonus of sympathy and knowledge of the social totality on the one hand and of class reconfirmation and the satisfactions of the bourgeois order on the other. The deeper class impulse in naturalism, indeed, which stimulated both of these reflexes simultaneously, was the fundamental petty-bourgeois terror of proletarianization, of slipping down the class ladder, of falling from a secure yet perpetually menaced middle-class "respectability" and "decency" back down into a proletarian space fantasized both in terms of filth and animality and also of insecure wage work. Its visions of misery were above all marked by the conviction that this condition was irrevocable, that once you lose your grip and drop down into this social space there is no climbing back and no return, no social salvation and no release or escape, no issue. There is of course a very real truth about this feeling in all the stages of capitalist society, where the old maxim about to him that has and from him that has not remains in force; but in the naturalist period, the late nineteenth century, the social fact was also a very powerful ideological fantasy, which could be appropriated and pressed into the service of a variety of other political uses and abuses.

Cyberpunk entertains a family likeness with all this, but with enormous structural and ideological modifications, of which the most fundamental seems to be the evaporation of a certain Otherness from this picture. The naturalist underclasses were always irredeemably other from ourselves, the bourgeois readers: we had the thrill of seeing through their eyes and living life through in their skins for a provisional and fictional proxy period, only to wake up again in the reassurance of our own. I think it could be argued in a variety of ways that one of the basic structural features of postmodernity lies in the weakening if not the outright disappearance of just this category of otherness and terrifying specieslike difference. I've observed above, indeed, that the precondition for what is sometimes called the politics of difference (or in other words micro- or small group politics today) is very precisely this universal weakening and sapping of real and objective difference on a global scale. It may also be suggested that this development—sometimes called democratization and that I prefer to call plebeianization (a good and more Brechtian word for it)—also has serious consequences for any philosophical arguments based on the opposition between Reason and unreason or the irrational (these last being categories of radical difference). It has above all welcome consequences for the age-old ethical and repressive categories of good and evil— where virtually in advance good is a category of the dominant group and evil a category of otherness—but which the new developments ought to go a certain way toward eradicating.

The proletarian, the lumpen, and their cousins the urban criminal (male) and prostitute (female)—these secure characters of the older bourgeois and naturalist imaginary representation of society—have today, in postmodernity and cyberpunk, given way to a youth culture in which the urban punks are merely the opposite numbers to the business yuppies, and in which city space is no longer so profoundly marked by the radical otherness of the older moment. There is now a circulation and recirculation possible between the underworld and the overworld of high-rent condos and lofts: falling from the latter into the former is no longer so absolute and irrevocable a disaster, above all since, offering a knowledge of what used to be called the streets, it can be useful for survival in the unimaginable spaces of corporate and bureaucratic decision (at least in the imagination of postmodern society and culture). But the crucial difference is that, in the postmodern view, you can return from the lower depths; a corporate comeback is possible and conceivable, something that would have been unthinkable and unrepresentable in the naturalist moment of mature capital (although perhaps not in the early capitalist fairy tales of a Balzac).

One would suppose then that with such a momentous transformation in social space and in the social imaginary as we witness with this enfeeblement if not extinction of the category of Otherness, the tasks of architecture (and of urbanism) would necessarily also find themselves modified, perhaps in unforeseeable and unexpected ways. The types of problems posed by the dilemmas of the naturalist moment with its class nightmares presumably involved the construction of a kind of private bourgeois space secure for the Other (perhaps Frank Lloyd Wright can serve as an example of this ambition at its most intense); they also surely involved the sanitation of the city itself, the cleansing of those lower depths or spaces of radical otherness, of which Victor Hugo's *cour des miracles* (in *Notre Dame de Paris*) and Dickens's Tom-all-alone's (in *Bleak House*) remain the more memorable precursor figurations. That surgical excision and hygienic urban reconstruction can perhaps be schematically marked and pegged by some of the projects of Le Corbusier (although I should want to emphasize that since we have here to do with resolutions of contradictions, answers to questions, responses to situations, no single name is binding, and a whole range of modern artists can be seen to be reacting to this general situation in a variety of stylistically very diverse ways).

But we cannot move on to the spatial consequences of a modification of all this in architectural "dirty realism" until we turn to the second of my two headings under this particular topic—one that now demands a more philosophical account of this social and spatial development in terms of the end, in late capitalism, of civil society itself. The term (which goes in German under the less euphemistic designation of *bürgerliche Gesellschaft* or bourgeois society) came into currency to describe the new private spaces that capitalism opened up for its new dominant class; it was at one with the philosophical paradoxes, posed for virtually the first time in the history of human societies or modes of production, of an experience and a conception of a radically nonpublic and nonsocial space that was however produced socially and constituted an integral component in the functioning of this particular social formation. Bourgeois privacy had nothing in common with the private spaces of antiquity or with those nonsocial areas into which the individual could withdraw, as a relief from the social and the public, in the great non-Western civilizations. It therefore tended to generate a whole range of dualistic antinomies, mostly concerned with the defense and definition of the private and the nonsocial as such but also, more rarely, as in Hannah Arendt, turning on the contamination of public space and public life that the new historical dualism brought equally with it. Like all dualisms, that now classical one between public and private cannot be resolved, except by disappearing into the past. What a more recent and perhaps more modernist social experience has brought with it is at least its complexification by two new kinds of space that did not compute in the older paradigm that opposed the public realm to the family and the home: these new spaces are the space of work (seemingly public, yet owned by private individuals); and the space of the street, henceforth called daily life or the everyday, the quotidian, which is fully as much a sign of the breakup of the private and the personal as it is of the emergence of consumption and commodification over against the public realm itself.

It is interesting to note that in Eastern Europe—despite the evidence of a vigorous but small bourgeois culture in Tsarist Russia, not to speak of the Central European countries—political reflection seems today to turn on this very issue of civil society: the dominant forces in these countries, after the liquidation of the Stalinist apparatus, tend to formulate their problems in terms of the failure to constitute civil society in the first place, thereby foreseeing a program that might, after the end of the construction of socialism, be characterized as the construction of civil society itself. I am not sure however, whether, in either Hegel's or Marx's sense, "civil society" is something that can be thus constructed. At any rate if in the mind of the Eastern reformers this project has something to do with catching up with the West, then unfortunately what needs to be pointed out is that the West is even more advanced than that by now, and that after our own period of civil society, what we are now witnessing in the United States, if not yet in a united Europe or Japan, is its wholesale liquidation. But we do not yet have the terms and categories ready to describe what succeeds civil society as such, when the latter's collapse is not a regression but rather the accompaniment of an even more advanced form of economic development. In my opinion, then, the visionary exploration of cyberpunk and so-called dirty realism provisionally occupies the place that may eventually be occupied by a full-dress theory of what follows civil society. This is also, however, why our own evocation of this new space will necessarily remained locked into the use of older words, such as public and private, which must be used against each other in a kind of self-problematizing way.

We must think of the space of dirty realism as a collective built space, in which the opposition between inside and outside is annulled. This accounts, among other things, or so it seems to me, for the Japanese allusions in films like *Blade Runner* (where Los Angeles seems to have migrated to the other side of the Pacific rim), or in Gibson's novels. Indeed, it seems plausible that as with Elizabethan visions of Spain, or the Soviet Union for us yesterday, the now obligatory Japanese reference also marks the obsession with the great Other, who is perhaps our own future rather than our past, the putative winner in the coming struggle—whom we therefore compulsively imitate, hoping that thereby the inner mind-set of the victorious other will be transferred to us along with the externals. It does not seem superfluous to add that the now notorious readaptation

of Hegel's end of history was passed on down to us by way of a fateful footnote in Kojève, which explicitly glosses this idea with Japan. It is therefore Japan that is somehow the "end of history" in store for us—and Japanese space, now obscurely valorized by our own anxieties, would seem to share in the general fascination and to project messages much more elaborate than the merely architectural.

The fantasy of dirty realism, indeed, draws strongly on the way in which, in parts of Tokyo, the street is somehow inside, so that the city as a whole, which has no profile, becomes one immense amorphous unrepresentable container that realizes the essence of the geodesic dome without the dome itself, and more conceptually than this distracting external figure ever could. Meanwhile, the echo of this macrophenomenon within, in the parts or microstructures, does not, I believe, take place in the hotels as with us: rather, in the department stores, which are open emporia in which one finds food markets, theaters, bookstores, and all kinds of other specialized services, run together in a fashion that surely derives ultimately and historically from the great open-air markets or bazaars of the East and of precapitalist modes of production. Here they form a new spatial and cultural entity, of which, in the West, only the French hypermarchés give any idea. Perhaps indeed such new forms—which cannot under any circumstances be grasped as regressions, or as some Spenglerian overwhelming of Europe by Asia—represent an overleaping and a dialectic whereby the postmodern formal and spatial needs of late capitalism demand the infusion and the supplement of the precapitalist: not the tribal archaic, as in the early modern, nor the forms of antiquity, as in neoclassicism, nor the feudal, as in the Gothic revival, but now the great non-Western "civilizations" (otherwise known as the Asiatic mode, or so-called oriental despotism).

At any rate the *Blade Runner* syndrome is just that: the interfusion of crowds of people among a high technological bazaar with its multitudinous nodal points, all of it sealed into an inside without an outside, which thereby intensifies the formerly urban to the point of becoming the unmappable system of late capitalism itself. Now it is the abstract system and its interrelations that are the outside: the former dome, the former city, beyond which no subject position is available, so that it cannot be inspected as a thing in its own right, although it is certainly a totality.

In contrast, we have the Western notion of movable compartments and rebuildable inner spaces, provisional rooms that are broken down and replaced by others at will; on the idea of the shed, into which you "put your stuff," as Gehry says, congregating your screens and furniture in one part of the warehouse space, and piling up boxes in the others—essentially individualistic visions and conceptions of some still inner space. It is only with the collectivization of that vision in cyberpunk and its deployment over an entire formerly urban area that something new begins to emerge, which we will call dirty realism and whose relationship to some putative end of civil society I mean to argue.

Dirty here means the collective as such, the traces of mass, anonymous living and using. The traditional values of privacy have disappeared, nor do we any longer approach this collective mass with the stark terror of the earlier inner-directed bourgeois individuals, for whom the multitude threatened a fall, as in naturalism, where collective space seemed radically unclean in the anthropological sense (rather than dirty, a somewhat more informal word that includes its own libidinal connotations). But the end of civil society is also betokened by the disappearance of public space as such: the end of the civic, for example, and of official government, which now dissolves back into the private networks of corruption and informal clan relationships. But since business is "private" in the juridical sense, then at that point its governments also become private; indeed, to return to Japan for one last time, van Wolferén argues that there is no Japanese government in any Western sense (despite the appearances) and that the Japanese corporations have their unique methods of directing the general drift of the national policy.

What now takes the place of the opposition between private and public? is there some intermediate zone between the two that survives, and how today to theorize the everyday or daily life, or the street, as one candidate for such an intermediary position? I believe that it is useful to think of the new space along the lines of a no-man's-land, not merely of warfare as such but of all previous traditional forms of boundaries (the paradox being that the category of boundary has in this situation disappeared). Spatially, this can be imagined as something in which neither private property nor public law exists. I think of a few literary analogies: Raymond Chandler's remark somewhere that when you enter a police station you pass into a space beyond the law; but even more strongly an episode in

one of John Le Carré's novels in which the characters meet in
a space beneath the Berlin wall, a space beyond all national or
political jurisdiction, in which the worst crimes can be committed with impunity and in which indeed the very social
persona itself dissolves. But such conceptions of the no-man's-
land are not altogether to be taken as nightmares; they do not,
as I tried to suggest earlier, have any of the bleak otherness of
the classical dystopian fantasy, and the very freedom from state
terror lends the violence of the no-man's-land the value of a
distinctive kind of praxis, excitement rather than fear—the
space of adventure that replaces the old medieval landscape of
romance with a fully built and posturban infinite space, where
corporate property has somehow abolished the older individual
private property without becoming public.

2

We may now continue our demonstration of the implications
of the semiotic square and its combinations and permutations
by picking up the destiny—in the postmodern era—of that
other component of the high modernist impulse, which was
identified as innovation, or the desire called the Novum. The
art generated by this particular pole will presumably project
an aesthetic that wishes to make a radical break, which stands
in principled opposition to the complacencies of replication,
and that somehow continues to identify its formal innovations
with a kind of protopolitics in the most general cultural or
philosophical sense: formalism in the strong sense, then (what
kind of smile is one supposed to wear when one says that?),
the Mallarmean approach to cultural politics if not to the
politics of culture. Actually, Mallarmé's own cultural politics,
based on Wagner—the conception of the Book of the World
as a sacred text, to be read to the initiate by secular officiants,
in a social ceremony dedicated to the regeneration of the
collectivity—was not much different from that more general

modernist conception of a Utopian totality-enclave within the real that I have characterized earlier. Meanwhile the architectural allusions to Mallarmé tend rather to dwell on the glacial emptiness of his "pure" forms, whereupon the reference to Mies becomes well-nigh obligatory and unavoidable. But any discussion of this kind of formal "nothingness" (the formal idea of writing a book "about nothing" was as we have seen Flaubert's, in the generation that preceded Mallarmé's own; the latter seems rather to have been a Hegelian and a proto-existentialist) needs to discuss the status of individual objects or items in the empty rooms of these poems and in particular the category of contingency that governs their status (it is more obvious in the great long poem about chance and a roll of the dice). Items: a curtain blowing in what is not even a window but only a window frame, and thus the very abstraction or hypothesis of empty form or syntax itself; a rose, or its absence, in the gesture of blossoming emergence into being— these stark objects rattle around in the formality of the late sonnets like meaningless words. Indeed, they have as their allegory the "ptyx," a kind of container the dead Master has gone to the river Styx to look for, which is to say a meaningless sound (chosen for the rhyme) whose henceforth Mallarmean meaning the rest of the sonnet has ended up constructing around it, filling its empty vase-ness with the merely grammatical meaning of the sentence in which it is housed. These radically isolated objects, then, demand the construction of a verbal "context" in order to replace that absent "real" ground or context from whose omission they suffer.

One wants to think this receding of a context or ground as a historical event, which has something to do with the seeming arbitrariness and optionality of the new built environment. A former nature ensured the look of necessity in the densely jumbled clods that filled its various eco-niches; but the gadgets and products of the industrial city can go anywhere. The isolated items then one by one are absolute contingency: each is the very form of unjustifiability itself, which is to say, of meaninglessness; nothing productive can come of any of them, not even a properly metaphysical experience, so trivial are they one by one and ready for the generational bonfire in which we dispose of the trinkets and furnishings of the newly departed. The surrealists, however, hunted those inexplicable trinkets down one by one in the flea markets; the stark isolation of each was for them an occasion for the flooding of libidinal investment, and the rising, like steam, of urban mystery: exhibits for defense or prosecution in the great unconscious crimes whose illustrations were as exciting as the pictures in dime novels or police weeklies. Nothing of the sort in Mallarmé, where even the "beauty" of the objects—of the absent flower, for example—is so cloying and fin de siècle as to designate itself as pure image, to derealize its own tawdriness as a shred of matter seen. The Mallarmean items would have to wait a long time for an aesthetic to crystalize around them, which could not be a surrealist one: I think, for example, of everything striking in *Twin Peaks* that derives essentially from the isolation of its props—the talking log, for one, but also everything else that looks like a clue, whatever the camera approaches in its nondelirious non-oneiric logic and renders in its false color. The characters are also a collection of this random type, and the ostentatious "Americanness" is neutrally quoted in the same way, as the meaninglessness of a mass-produced item taken all by itself. Lynch comes out of the image-stream on the other side of mass production; in him the pure Mallarmean fountain is tasteless and non-nourishing, a synthetic liquid that does not even have a medicinal flavor to identify it. But in visual narrative of this kind, space and its contents, depth, the built environment, and the very hut of being itself, are all drawn inside out onto the screen and transcoded into so many image-items.

Mallarmé's items, however, were still housed in empty rooms; and it must now be a question what those rooms might look like that are made to do justice to the radicality of the isolated items—an aesthetic dilemma, insofar as they cannot be items themselves, they must house the visual and therefore transcend it like its syntax. For another generation, Mies was thought to have provided that, and glass and frame transparency was the way in which the Mallarmean room was thought. But something new enters the picture when the idea of syntax is itself revised. Mallarmé thought—or composed as though he thought—that the sentence itself was the supreme embodiment of absolute syntax and thereby offered the promise of some absolute closure: where the monad still sounded spatial, the absolute sentence buckles its definitive buckle in a provisional time (which evades the ideology of the cyclical as well and foreshadows the more contemporary conception of the synchronic).

But if we begin to doubt syntax itself—to wonder whether its operations assure coherence and meaning, and to suspect that the very form of its necessary figures and tropes ensures their internal contradiction of each other—then a place is reached in which linguistic structuralism has already generated deconstruction out of itself. It is then famously also a place in which spatial formalism is unable to rest calmly within itself but begins to generate a nonstructural negation of its own system, a development that in the case of Peter Eisenman has won his work the unlovely qualification of "deconstructionist": a move—not beyond formalism and rationalism, exactly, but against formalism and rationalism undermined by their own weapons and undone in a formalist and rationalist manner. The motivation of the device, here, remains philosophical; it is formulated in terms of the critique of humanism and of anthropocentrism (in other words of a worldview or lived, preconscious philosophy):

> Though Freud's exposition of the unconscious rendered this
> naive anthropocentric view forever untenable, its roots

persist in the architecture of today. The issues of presence and origin are central to the question of anthropocentrism. In order to effect a response in architecture to this new circumstance of man, this project proposes to employ an *other* discourse, one which attempts to eschew the anthropocentric organising principles of presence and origin.

This passage derives, to be sure, from a somewhat later stage in Eisenman's own development (the one primarily of interest to us here), a stage in which temporal layers and levels have come to add content to the pure and contradictory geometric syntax of Houses VI and X in much the same way that the color schemes of the Romeo and Juliet project (from which the quote was taken) are superimposed on the black-and-white of the axonometric figures.

I raise the matter of the philosophical program of the "deconstructionist" period in order to clarify Eisenman's relationship with high modernism, whose fundamental value of Innovation is certainly rehearsed here. It no longer proposes the achievement of a vivid new unique personal style in the banal sense of a style immediately distinctive, which sets you off from the older generation—that is only the most obvious and aesthetic form taken by the high modernist logic of innovation, and the category of style it invents and deploys would in itself be enough to alert us to its incompatibility with this particular postcontemporary artist whose rational or geometric formalism is already a repudiation of personal style in that warm visceral sense, fully as much as his antihumanism explicitly identifies and excludes it.

But the Novum can take many forms. The notion of the revolutionary break is yet another and not the most negligible of them; it can be realized on whatever level, from politics to philosophy. In this purely formal sense, it is all one whether you have in mind a loathing for the overstuffed interiors of Victorian private life and wish to abolish that, in the name of a proletarian way with machinery and praxis, or in the name of some vitalism à la D. H. Lawrence; or whether you think that it is the intellectual or spiritual formation of the world's current generation that is at fault—their metaphysics or their relationship to the question of being, their ideological values, their episteme, the quality of their consciousness, their mental equipment, or the very shape of their being-in-the-world. In all these different configurations, materialist and idealist alike, what counts is the will to some kind of absolute break with all that, or even only the possibility of forming the idea of the very possibility of such a break. That breath of a thought, possibility of a possibility, is enough to ground the notion of the modern as some radical difference with what has gone before; and the great antimetaphysical project remains in that sense, even residually, modern. It is in any case repudiated by a variety of ideological postmodernisms, for which, in their very different ways, it is crucial to refuse the notion of radical change, historical difference, revolution, the break itself (even as a concept).

But obviously, like Koolhaas, Eisenman is more and other than a residual modernist, not even a late modernist of the Jencks type; it therefore becomes crucial to specify the other, nonmodernist component of his aesthetic mode. We have in fact made a beginning on that specification with our discussion of the objects and the items: to anticipate, these will become the pure disconnected "parts, elements, signifiers" of a more completely postmodern practice (and are designated as such in the appropriate corner of our semiotic square). But it is equally clear (at least a priori) that the category of the part or element cannot in Eisenman play the same role or occupy the same function that we have found it to do in the practice of a Koolhaas or as it can be anticipated to do in work like that of Michael Graves or Charles Moore.

The very formalism of Eisenman's first period suggests that the part qua part will have been repressed in this form and will only emerge in the more generalized position of content as such, where it is not particularly identified with any specific objects or ornaments nor is it to be thought of as raw material either in any conventional sense. "Content," for the most abstract of all buildings (that is to say, for whatever idea we might achieve of such a building), would necessarily and stubbornly remain the ineradicability of what is now called site, and to put it this way is to open up a fundamental (and historically new), properly postmodern possibility, that even site itself can be done away with. This should not be taken too rapidly as an ecological truth: for its ecological form (which is very real indeed, and chilling enough) needs to be ranged under a larger diagnostic rubric in order to avoid the still humanist pathos of the denunciation of the "domination of nature," the rape of and will to power over the earth itself. Ecological damage in that sense is a subset of capitalist fungibility in general: the technological transformation of all forms of ground and raw material, including space itself, into the indifferent materials of commodification and the purely formal occasions for profit. We need rather to take into consideration the possibility that the renewed attention to the problem of the site is itself a function of the imminent extinction of the very category in question: an urgency and a desperation that then washes back over this theme to lend it a kind of second-degree historical content in its own right, the return of "content" itself as a new event.

Site could not, clearly, have been absent from Eisenman's earlier, more "formalist" moment: indeed, he goes to some lengths to explain how, in House X, "site was a major consideration," owing to the automative relationship between this suburban house and the city, as a result of which "the house became—for the first time in my work—a model of the reality of car/house seen as part of the total fabric of urbanism, an icon of that relationship." (154) Here, significantly, a part/whole relationship is rewritten allegorically rather than functionally, as a mere synechdoche; and the discussion of the site in terms of the structural relationship of city to suburb precedes its evocation in purely physical terms ("a fairly steep continuous slope running downhill from south to north," and so on). These two developments are in reality the same: the allegory is at one with the overleaping of place into space, with the mapping of the house in terms of the absent geopolitical axis of country and city rather than the perceptual and phenomenological, experiential, data of the isolated plot of land.

I take it for granted that some form of allegory has always been implicit in architecture as such, although in its classical forms perhaps so entangled with the immediacies of perception that its filigrain could not be detected: thus, it is difficult, when it is a question of building along the line of a hill, to distinguish between the physical requirements of the site and a wall or plumb line that necessarily alludes to the ridge, repeating and reproducing its specific orientation. Such difficulties are compounded by the multiple echoes the site leaves within the construct, which must nonetheless as they grow more numerous and complex separate themselves from sheer contiguity to become a kind of idea or even a meaning. To lean against a rise is to turn a natural accident into a support and the approach to a mode of dwelling; to multiply such attitudes is to produce a veritable mimesis of leaning that then becomes endowed with a semi-autonomous meaning of its own, or at least gradually comes to ask for interpretation. I am struck by the omnipresence of these allegorical patterns in contemporary architecture (often termed "analogies"), and even more by the way in which they are taken for granted, as the inevitable fabric of the thing. But if one wanted to resist the anthropomorphic and humanism, would this not offer a different but no less dramatic starting point—a principled effort to do away with just such an allegorical infrastructure, and to imagine an architecture capable of doing without such allusions and such geographical mimetisms?

Eisenman's earlier houses were generally, as I understand it, taken to have attempted just that, a kind of antifoundationalism in the philosophy of construction. Nor am I probably alone in seeing his later trajectory as exemplary of the various passages out of high structuralism toward the reinvention of this or that kind of content, which structuralist formalism began to demand like a chemical craving. Many of these returns from formalism found an easy missing content in psychoanalysis, which seems also to have played a significant role in Eisenman's development. Marxism meanwhile offered a more demanding "absolute formalism," while deconstruction, as we have seen, also put a "post" to structuralism in its commitment to the implacable foregrounding of the metaphysical structure of modern thought and consciousness.

As Eisenman's association with Derrida is more than well-known and the analogies between this architecture and philosophical deconstruction have been so often rehearsed, it may not seem altogether abusive to experiment with a somewhat different analogy and to confront Eisenman's practice with another philosophical work of the same period, which has not yet I think been mentioned in its connection. Indeed, particularly in the light of the relationship between Derrida and Althusser, and in view of the more than occasional intersections between their thinking, it does not seem inappropriate to stage a discussion of the later buildings in terms of a once classical text from the now extinguished Althusserian canon: Pierre Macherey's *Towards a Theory of Literary Production* (1966), the major aesthetic contribution of Althusserianism, and a work that has, particularly via Eagleton's reading of it, known some influence in England and to a lesser degree in the United States.

The first half of this book develops a polemic against naive or referential reading, of a type long since familiar here as long ago as the New Criticism: it is with the later, analytical chapters that we now rather have to do here, whose practice seems to me to offer a method and a model of far greater originality and interest.

Those chapters, which deal unevenly with Borges and Jules Verne, with Balzac's novel *The Peasants,* and with Lenin's views on Tolstoy, offer readings that express a polemic, but also an experiential, feeling that the "work of art" as such is not the organic unity it normally passes itself off as being: that its unity is indeed a sham and a makeshift, if not very precisely a kind of ideology in its own right (this is a position that Eagleton's related *Criticism and Ideology* has very strongly defended in the English-language critical tradition). The work, then—the *former* work—is rather to be seen as an act whereby a batch of disparate materials—a kind of lumber room of all kinds of different contents, partial forms, linguistic phenomena, social and psychological raw material, semi-autonomous ideological fantasies, local period concepts, scientific spare parts, and random topical themes—are forcibly yoked together and fused by the power of aesthetic ideology into what looks like an organic whole. What used to be considered a "work" therefore is now to be treated as best as a kind of anthology of disconnected parts and pieces and at worst as a kind of dumping ground for objective spirit.

Yet the disparate raw materials are all clearly in one way or another social and historical: they come from someplace real, they bear, even cold, the traces of ancient struggles and of a once historical emergence. This is why the tension between such seemingly unrelated levels and building materials can be rewritten in the strong forms of the antinomy if not the contradiction itself. From the Machereyan standpoint, then, the incompatibility between, say, this or that sentimental experience that the novel inscribes and this or that anecdotal unit, this or that mode of stylistic formulation—an incompati-

bility potentially so great as to show up as a kind of jarring
wrong note on the very surface of the text—such incompatibility is now to be read as a sign and symptom of some deeper
historical and social contradiction that it is the business of the
analyst to bring to light.

But if that is the case, then we must now, in a second
moment, reevaluate the act of aesthetic reunification denounced a moment ago. Freud indeed often spoke of what he
called the "secondary elaboration" of the dream process,
wherein the disparate wish-fulfillments and the random content of the nascent dream were then sewn and resewn together
in a multiplication of ornamental interrelations that the earliest
translators significantly called "overdetermination." This process of aesthetic and formal unification after the fact—getting
rid of the loose threads, making up plausible connections
where none existed before, rationalizing the coexistence of the
different materials in a secondary and misleading way—this is
surely very close to what Macherey and Eagleton have in
mind, save for the consequence that if the disrelation of the
materials is here seen as a contradiction, then the smoothing
over of those incommensurabilities and the forging of something that looks unified must now be seen as more than a mere
aesthetic act. It is also an ideological one, and aims at nothing
less than the resolution of the contradiction itself. Organic
form thereby reacquires its value as a social and protopolitical
act. On the other hand, it should also be stressed that from
the standpoint of Machereyan analysis, this act remains ambiguous, and must continue to be readable in two distinct and
antithetical ways: it is seen as unifying the material and resolv-
ing the contradictions by papering them over with form,
but on the other hand the analysis itself demonstrates that
contradictions can never be resolved and that the "work"
itself—the former work—is for all that nothing but a coexistence of discontinuous materials.

Something like this seems to me to be happening in the

The Constraints

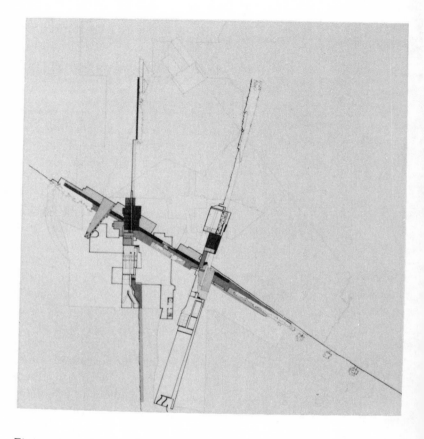

Eisenman projects, where a *layering*—literally reified or published for us in the Romeo and Juliet box, with its superimposed transparencies—marks the irreducibility of each of the
levels to each other. This is dramatized in the superimpositions
of the Long Beach University Art Museum project, for example, in the incompatibility between the coordinates of various
time zones,

beginning with the settlement of California in 1849, the
creation of the campus in 1949, and the projected "redis-

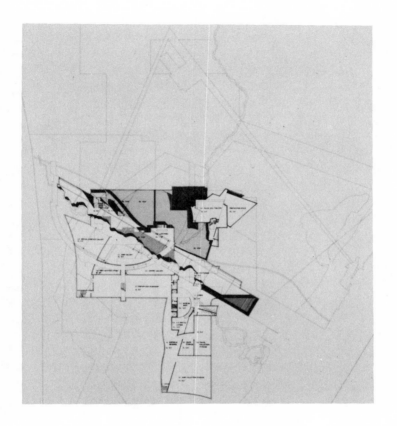

covery" of the museum in the year 2049. The idea was to imagine the site in the year 2049, 100 years after the founding of the university, and 200 years after the period of the gold rush.

The building takes its form from the overlapping registration of several maps: of the ranch that once existed on the site, the site of the campus, and the changing configurations of fault lines, a river, a channel, and the coastline. They are combined in such a way that none of the notations takes precedence over any other, and so as to textualize

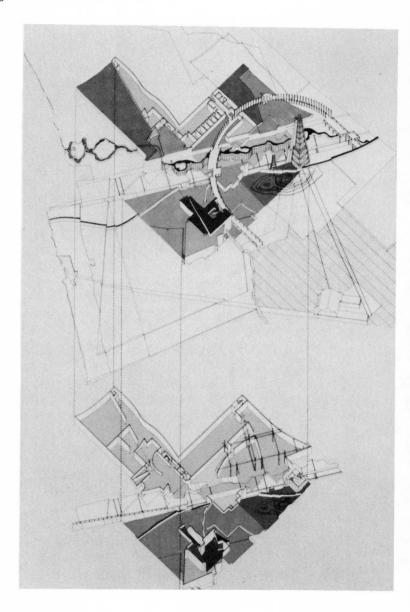

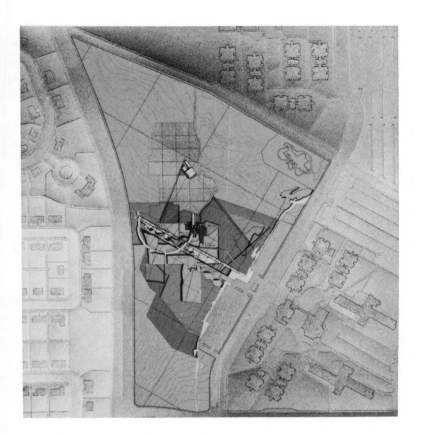

coincidental overlaps by subjective interpretations. These "superpositions" reveal analogical relationships that were obscured when some notations, such as social delineations, were accorded more importance. For example, the relationship of the channel at the northern edge of the museum site is similar to the relationship of the river to the entire campus site. Thus, the building could be seen as an archeological artifact, a palimpsest both of its formation and of its superposed "histories."

In areas, the stone of the building bears the mark of a once existing riverbed, or the outline of former ranch boundaries, always overlaid with similar textual marks of fictive conditions. Thus the stone of this architecture, instead of "configurating" an "image" of a museum, records the traces of a lost and a future history. The different historical layers and shifts could be understood as marks of intelligence, glimpses of the way a culture organized itself. In this sense architecture becomes the intervention into and the invention of stories, and this project represents a story about Long Beach that is different from those which have spoken for it previously. (*Recent Projects,* 25)

The formal paradox emerges classically in the flipover from description to prescription, from analysis to fresh production, and can be articulated in terms of the problem of the unified work. If that was always a lie to begin with and the work never was unified, then if you know that and still want to produce a work of your own, do you produce random fragments and discontinuous remains, or do you first imagine a unified thing and then deconstruct yourself? What strikes me in all Eisenman's recent projects is the return of history, via the discontinuities of the site itself: the layerings are now historical, ghosts of various pasts, presents, and futures, which may in fact be alternate worlds but whose tensions and incompatibilities are all mediated through some larger absent cause, which is History itself.

If so, it is a different quality of history than what high modernism claimed to supply: cleanly fictive pasts, as surgical as the transparencies of the Romeo and Juliet box, without anything of the archaic shadows of that "well of the past" that overflows like the periodicity of the Nile in the opening Prelude to Thomas Mann's *Joseph* tetralogy, bottomless, each

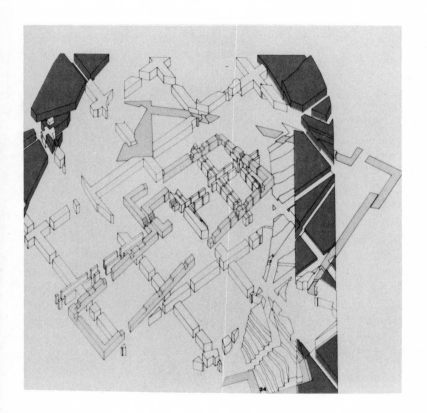

deeper memory proving to be a "time-coulisse" behind which, like a screen, some yet deeper layer of the older and earlier lies concealed. *"Was aber ist die Zeit?"* No origin either, this modernist "time sense"—already a virtually Althusserian "always-already" about which it is not the reality of the concept but the passion for it, in the modernist period, that demands some accounting. (We wiser postmoderns know already what Norman Holland pointed out so long ago—about "myth criticism"—that a text does not yield a "myth-effect" unless it is marked that way in advance, suggestively, like directions on a package.) Still, even the relatively postmodern revel in their

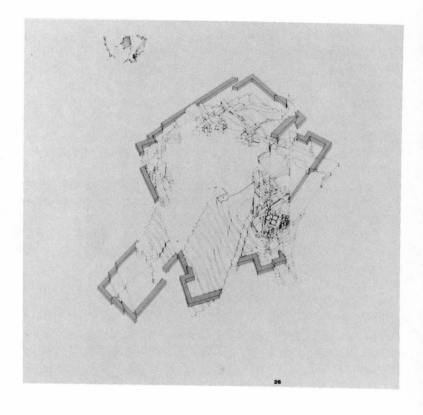

own forms of the desire called the deep past: as witness Lucy Lippard's striking *Overlay,* in which the affinities and intricate retroactivities between archaic tribal art of various kinds and post-Smithson conceptuality are richly documented: although the crucial nuance must be resonated, that not some thrilling Jungian base note is demanded of these dolmens and cave paintings today, but rather, for Lippard, the communal and collective social life that speaks through them and that we continue, ever so faintly, to hear, in our postindividual solitude.

The temptation is great to assimilate something of Eisenman

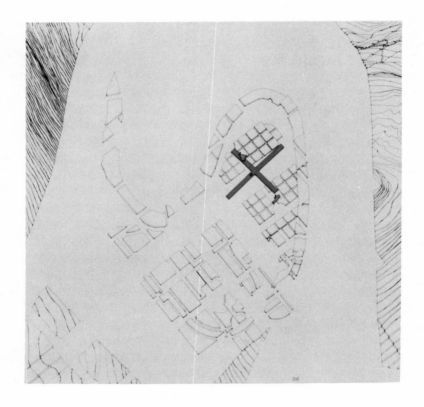

to contemporary science fiction (Kenneth Frampton does not altogether resist it in his critical essay, in *Recent Projects,* adducing in addition the "disturbing" allusion to Edward Albee's uncanny play *Tiny Alice*); the Long Beach project in particular can trigger associations with Ballard (and his own ready-made California ruins) that are perhaps a little too apocalyptic (and also too narrative) for this orthogonal architecture. The latter's primal splitting of the atom seems to lie in the fracturing of the cube into so many hollowed el-blocks, which are not merely systematically rearranged (in an interminable geometrical permutation) but ultimately held apart and wedged open

by a great, nameless, cagelike force, an empty wedge that seems already allegorical (in a somewhat different sense from our use here) of that "betweenness" that Eisenman evokes as a kind of third party to his various dualisms. The full spatial enactment and embodiment of this primal drama is then exhibited in the Wexner Center itself (Ohio State University, Columbus), where ready-made mint ruins ("old" battlements, earthworks, armories) spring into life around the irresistible movement of the glass scaffolding that is driven slantways through them.

Here we return again to the superposition of grids, of

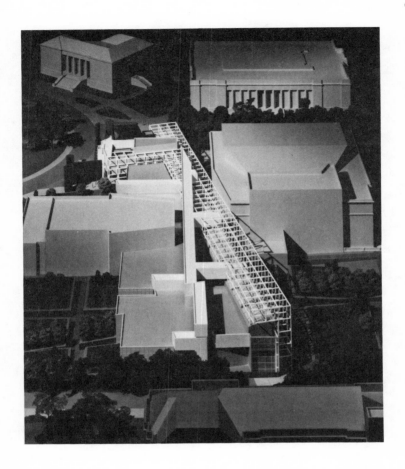

which the Wexner Center wedge is a dramatic exemplar, not least because it may correspond to an altogether fictive set of coordinates. It is indeed from this possibility of multiple grids in an articulated simultaneity that the possibilities of Eisenman's new kind of historical projection derive. But the grids also return us to that other primal dilemma of all modern architecture, which is the incompatibility of a focus on the individual building (the individual architectural "work of art") and that on the city itself or the urban "fabric" (no matter that this dilemma is itself historically generated by a private property system). Grids clearly correspond to precisely that fabric into which, with vernacular fluency, we have seen Venturi suggest that we insert ourselves: and to that heterogeneous macrocosm of the urban that it became the vocation of Koolhaas's enormous microcosms to replicate like so many self-sufficient monads. Eisenman's Ohio State version of a formal response (for one does not "solve" a form-problem like this, which is an irresolvable contradiction, rather one acknowledges it ad hoc in some new form-producing way) is suggestively characterized by Rafael Moneo as follows:

> The entire construction becomes a fragment of a city and, as a consequence, it loses the unitary and synthetic image that building once had. Here, structures and grids are what our eyes see rather than references to figural aspects which used to characterize buildings. This most probably is purposefully sought. Eisenman Trott's architecture emerges as an architectural phenomenon without assuming the condition of a building. *(El Croquis, 57)*

"Without assuming the condition of a building." These altogether remarkable words suddenly join the ground-bass of the deepest vocations of all the modern arts: as Roland Barthes once put it, to put off as long as possible the status of the finished work, of what, as a reified object, was then at once by definition over and done with: "to prolong that penumbral existence, as in a waiting room," between Art as such and the individual work. Identification with the various grids now for one long moment makes this possible for Eisenman as well, but generates some supplementary problems in its turn.

For nothing could be more congenial, or so it might seem, to the amateur of undecideability, than the multiple and incompatible "readings" given off by each of these optional grids in turn. What threatens this innocent pleasure is the nostalgia for harmony implicit in all such pluralism (the very fact of naming the situation and promising to turn it into a method is a symptom of "humanism" and of the promise that the incompatibles will all on the other side of the rainbow eventually be reconciled): in this case, it is Gestalt psychology that menaces otherwise scandalous dualisms and offers to turn them back into the placid Janus-faced natural alternation of the rabbit and its Other.

I believe that Eisenman's specific new historicity is to be grasped as a response to this immediate form-problem: seen in this way, it is not a stylistic option or embellishment but an unavoidable next move. He calls this first of all "scaling," a word presumably derived from Mandelbrot and chaos theory (in which infinite enlargements and reductions infallibly repeat the "self-same" constitutive irregularities and anomalies); in my view, however, it is the "motivation" by way of the most postcontemporary science that is optional. In reality scaling achieves something more fundamental and formal: namely, to unwedge multiple readings from the Gestalt, by projecting the lines of force of the synchronic (the grids) onto any number of diachronic axes. Scaling is therefore the equivalent in the realm of "scale" itself, or dimension, of what the various color schemes of the Romeo and Juliet box offered to model in the realm of temporality: "present elements (in color), elements of memory (in grey), and elements of immanence (in white)" (*Moving Arrows,* plate 7)—in fact, the very forces Raymond Williams tried to X-ray out of actuality with his notions of the "residual" and the "emergent."

In the Romeo and Juliet box, indeed, both these processes are at work simultaneously, offering an interplay of aesthetic perceptions more complex than anything since Schoenberg's *Klangfarbenmelodie,* in which the sequence of specific instruments (flute, drum, string, trumpets) was rigorously coded according to notes in the theme, such that the recurrence of that particular sequence thus also unexpectedly constituted a repetition, but in some other dimension of the work altogether.

Scaling is also appealed to, in Eisenman, as a way of "destabilizing" narrative, or at least "the traditional idea of what is an architectural narrative" (*Recent Projects* 58): but the context makes it clear he has in mind all the stale narrativities still implicit in the various architectural metaphors—something it was the historical merit of his own purism to have shown up, and another reason why one should hesitate before receiving the various themes of "ruin" here in some more properly Science-Fictional way (it being understood that SF is taken here as a signal historical achievement, of the rarest kind, and not a high-cultural reproach). But the words *traditional idea of* authorize us to suppose that new kinds of narratives are then not altogether undesirable or impossible; and I will indeed take the Eisenman dimensional effect (still most programmatically visible in the Long Beach project) as just such a projection of a new kind of historical narrative, one in which the present invents its own past, much like Bertrand Russell's God, who created this present only a moment ago, with a wondrous craftsmanship that rendered all the "always-alreadies" and the temporal perspectives, the local and more distant depths of past in so uncanny and lifelike fashion that we are tempted to think it has been standing there for thousands of years. Postmodern historicity then immediately becomes self-conscious and modestly embarrassed about its achievement, which it protests ("following Nietzsche") to be only a fiction. But we need not make up our minds too hastily about that, since it may turn out that, if this is the only kind of historicity we can have, we will have more ambitious plans for it. I once found myself thinking that the postmodern "historical novel," with all its false chronologies and made-up chronicles and genealogies, constituted a referential use of fiction to free ourselves from the irrevocability of the "facts" of the history manuals and to institute a simultaneity of multiple worlds. Here the problem may be that of activating and deploying narrativities without ending up producing a single narrative object that would finally be "only that": "one recognizes in this project that architecture is about the telling of stories, and this stone text that is being written, this fiction, might tell a very different story about Long Beach than has ever been recorded before."

3

It will have been understood, as we now continue around the semiotic square to our final "type" or position, that the grids of the site and the geopolitical in general are what allow Eisenman his special way with the dilemma of whole and part, or totality and contents. To conceive the part as a grid, and the grid as part or element, is to make that provisional new coexistence possible that we call Eisenman's architecture. But as has also been seen, its other condition of possibility is that specifically modernist passion to cancel the unacceptable stereotypes and conventions of a dead past in order to bring something radically new into being. What now happens to the parts or components when that passion is also abdicated, along with the "aspiration to totality" that empowered a Koolhaas?

The answer need not be a privative one; indeed, I have come to think that several rather different kinds of answers are possible in this situation, which in this sense then characterizes postmodernism in its narrower and more exclusive sense (of what makes a heroic effort to eschew everything about the modern, from totality to innovation). The three variants are not only a function of the different ways in which the problem of the part is conceived; they also respond, even more funda-mentally, to the other term to be synthesized, the pole of replication, which clearly enough itself knows possibilities of variation. Thus, as a general "context," the object of replica-tion can be late modern everyday life in general as in Venturi (that is to say, U.S. urban life or "Las Vegas"); it can however also be constituted by the general field of what Benjamin designated by the term *mechanical reproduceability,* or in other words media culture. Finally (as in Critical Regionalism), it can be specifically inflected in the direction of a *foreign* culture (and perhaps even, in the perspective of cultural imperialism, a nonhegemonic foreign culture—or at least one that has some cultural and traditional stake in resisting the U.S. media variety).

The variations in both these poles suggest that the number of combinations possible is a good deal greater than the three variants identified here: but to do justice to the abstract possibilities would require a whole new combination scheme at this point and thus a whole new discussion; while these three at least have the virtue of existing, as genuine movements or currents (or in the case of Critical Regionalism, as a concept that seems to offer a coherent aesthetic and has been widely debated as such).

At any rate, the number of different positions both logically and ideologically possible in that principled negation of totality that emerges as a central issue here is very great and probably not to be reduced to that familiar litany of the Fragment and the fragmentary that appeals back, across the literary texts of Nietzsche, to those of the Schlegels and the first (Jena) Romanticism (but the role of both these literary moments in deconstruction, and particularly in the work of Paul de Man, reminds us of the rather different participation of this feature in our previous moment as well). Surely a variety of attitudes toward the "component" can be imagined here—decorations and floating signifiers fully as much as outright potsherds, part objects, neologisms, and assorted vocabulary, the contents of various kinds of tool kits, and even molecular by-products or waste; but the range of variations probably spans the great curve that leads from raw materials as such to modules, that is to say, from style to construction. Style and construction,

respectively, are indeed the dominants of the first two actual-
izations of this moment on which we will touch here: "postmodernism" and neorationalism, respectively, where postmodernism is clearly to be grasped in a more restricted, and indeed
more exclusively stylistic, sense than the more historical and
sociological one in which it has generally been used.

I mean here, in other words, that peculiarly lavish and
ornamental, decorative "style" that has seemed to many people
to embody what is quintessential about postmodernism in
general (its hedonism, its refusal of asceticism, or on the other
hand its frivolity and essential superficiality, depending on your
perspective) and that has latterly, after its great precursors
Venturi and Charles Moore, seemed to find its classical and
hegemonic embodiment in the work of Michael Graves. The
question of the part here—component, fragment, element, or
building block—seems dominant, well beyond the merely
"superficial" matter of "ornamentation" as such, insofar as,
particularly in the work of Moore and Graves, it is somehow
the empty or paradoxical relationship of the various parts to
each other that often seems to constitute the building as such.
Indeed, it has been observed how in such work the "various
elements—architrave, column, arch, order, lintel, dormer,
and dome—begin with the slow force of cosmological processes to flee each other in space, standing out from their
former supports, as it were, in free levitation" like "Dali's late
Christs hovering over the crosses they were nailed to, or
Magritte's men in bowler hats slowly descending from the
skies in the form of the raindrops that determined them to
wear their bowler hats and carry their umbrellas in the first
place."

This levitation—this strange afterlife in the void that is the
condition of a figure without ground—can be compared to the
organs that float within Koolhaas's cubic totalities; they can be
contrasted to the superimposed grids in Eisenman, which in
this respect might better be characterized as grounds without

a figure (and that have therefore been dialectically promoted to the status of figures in their own right). The figures of the stylistically postmodern suggest a cultural element that would be something like the collective or media unconscious through which such indigestible remnants float, along with the flags, the map of Italy, and other such public icons that indeed tend to reduce this implicit model of the public sphere (the Piazza d'Italia, in New Orleans) to its most impoverished and rudimentary Fourth of July American celebratory version. This is then to be sharply distinguished from the way in which the storehouse of forms and types is figured in Italian neorationalism, where it is clearly the history of architecture itself—identified with the whole classical history of Latin Christendom—that offers the limbo in which more properly architectural signifiers and part-objects wait in half-life for their resurrection at Aldo Rossi's hands.

Yet a certain libidinal restraint, which can indeed be prolonged on into asceticism or irony, marks a kinship between Rossi and Robert Venturi, who might in that respect—if Las Vegas were pronounced rational—be described as a kind of mass-cultural neorationalist whose respect for the coherence of that city fabric is no less than what is prescribed by the Italians for the much more ancient (and thus, alas, far more "high cultural") city fabric within which they must work, and whose manipulation of the pre-given components (of a *vernacular* in his case, rather than a typology) is equally self-effacing and deliberately undramatic. Both are then menaced by a certain breakdown of this repression or decorum: pressure, a swelling away at the paradigm, a kind of internal disquiet, can indeed be sensed in the rich materials and Kahn-like elegance of Venturi's Gordon Wu building at Princeton, while Rossi's Hotel Il Palazzo at Fukuoka comes close to a controlled delirium in the abnormal scale of its windowless green-and-orange facade, whose blank rows of columns simulate an enormous grave marker, while within a gilt hush glows within narrow spaces of great depth and height, like archaic recesses destined for obscure ritual uses: a building that would provide an excellent occasion for reflecting on the nature of the differences that separate the postmodernity of this particular fin de siècle from the decadence of the last one.

Not so paradoxically, it is in another field that we find the most interesting critical arguments against this particular practical strategy of foregrounding the part or component over against the former whole: the fact that this critique emerges from political philosophy, then, suggests some more general transferability of the present scheme to postmodern political practice and theory as well, which we will not, however, pursue further here. Ernesto Laclau and Chantal Mouffe's *Hegemony and Socialist Strategy,* indeed, is ideologically committed to the task of demonstrating the logical incoherence (as well as the politically debilitating effects) of various doctrines of totality or social closure (most of them taxed with Hegelian or Marxian affinities): their argument clearly places their text within the problematic mapped out by our use of the semiotic square. What is particularly relevant for us is their interesting critique of the rival critique of totality offered by the English political theorists Hindiss, Hirst, and Cutler. Laclau and Mouffe argue that by stigmatizing global conceptions of society and the economy in the name of their various (for Hindess, Hirst, and Cutler) not necessarily related parts—such as institutions, forms of organization, or agents—the notion of a preexisting unity finds itself simply transferred from the former whole to the former parts or elements or components:

> The notion of totality is here rejected by reference to the nonessential character of the links uniting the elements of the presumed totality. In this, we have no disagreements. But, once elements such as "institutions," "forms of organization," or "agents" have been specified, a question immediately arises. If these aggregates—by contrast with

> the totality—are considered legitimate objects of social theorization, must we conclude that the relations among the internal components of each of them are essential and necessary? If the answer is yes, we have clearly moved from an essentialism of the totality to an essentialism of the elements; we have merely replaced Spinoza with Leibniz, except that the role of God is no longer to establish harmony among the elements, but simply to secure their independence. (*Hegemony,* 103)

Replace the "institutions, forms of organization, or agents" of Hindess, Hirst, and Cutler with the architectural signifiers or types of stylistic postmodernism or neorationalism and a provocative analogy begins to develop, in which the "totalizing" coherence of the high modernist building is repudiated but not the formal autonomy of the parts and components that survive its disintegration. This seemingly logical objection might also go a certain way toward accounting for the kitsch effect of the quotation of preexisting smaller forms in this architecture—itself a function of the renunciation of the New or of Innovation. The aporia is not unlike that confronted by contemporary linguistics (particularly its Chomskyan form): all of the words and sentence structure of a given language preexist the individual speaker, who is nonetheless able to fashion out of them creative utterances never before spoken.

Nor is it clear whether the solution of Laclau and Mouffe themselves—their conception of an *articulation* as "a relation among elements such that their identity is modified as a result of the articulatory practice" (105)—can have any particular relevance or application in the architectural field: although if analogies can be established there, they would probably have more to do with Eisenman or Koolhaas (in their very different ways) than with the architectural movements in question in this particular semiotic quadrant.

As for the third movement associated with this final position, several paradoxes are associated with its identification and placement here. What Kenneth Frampton (following Tzonis and Lefaivre) calls Critical Regionalism, is for one thing virtually by definition not a movement: he himself calls it a "critical category oriented towards certain common features" ("Critical Regionalism" 326), but there seems no good reason for us not to go on to characterize it as an exemplar of that virtually extinct conceptual species, an *aesthetic,* for it is certain that Critical Regionalism knows, perhaps in untraditional proportions, the same fundamental tension between the descriptive and the prescriptive that marks all philosophical (but also all vanguard) aesthetics. Such systems—and it would be appropriate to limit its history as a project to the bourgeois era as such, from the mid-eighteenth to the mid-twentieth centuries—in effect seek, by describing the constitutive features of authentic works of art as they already exist, to suggest invariants and norms for the production of future works. To put it this way is to realize how unseasonable this project is today, and how unfashionable the very conception of aesthetics must be in an age of artistic nominalism and antinomianism. It can be argued that the "second modernism" of the avant-gardes represented any number of efforts to free art from aesthetics (I take this to be Peter Bürger's position in *Theory of the Avant-Garde*); it can also be argued that aesthetics emerges as a problematic with secular modernism, whose contradictions finally render it impossible (this would at least be one way of reading Adorno's *Aesthetic Theory*). Meanwhile, on any philosophical view, the totalizing normativity of this kind of traditional philosophical discourse is clearly very unpostmodern indeed: it sins against the poststructural and postmodern repudiation of the conception of a philosophical system, and is somehow un- and antitheoretical in its values and procedures (if one takes the position that what is called theory today, or "theoretical discourse," constitutes a displacement of traditional philosophy and a replacement of or substitute for it).

Yet it is equally clear, not merely that Frampton is aware of all this but also that a certain deliberate retrogression is built into the project itself where it is underscored by the slogan of an *arrière-garde* or rearguard action, whose untimely status is further emphasized by Frampton's insistence that whatever Critical Regionalism turns out to be, in its various regions of possibility, it must necessarily remain a "marginal practice" ("Critical Regionalism," 327).

But these features suggest a second paradox in any typology that associates the aesthetic of Critical Regionalism with the stylistic postmodernisms of the relevant (mainly North American) contemporary architects: for while it can be said that Critical Regionalism shares with them a systematic repudiation of certain essential traits of high modernism, it distinguishes itself by attempting at one and the same time to negate a whole series of postmodern negations of modernism as well, and can in some respects be seen as antimodern and antipostmodern simultaneously, in a "negation of the negation" that is far from returning us to our starting point or from making Critical Regionalism over into a belated form of modernism.

Such is for example very precisely the stand outlined here on the matter of the avant-garde, which remained, in high modernism, both Enlightenment and Utopian, sought to outtrump the vulgar bourgeois conception of progress, and retained the belief in the possibilities of a liberatory dimension to technology and scientific development. But the postcontemporary forms of such "progress," in global modernization, corporate hegemony, and the universal standardization of commodities and "life styles," are precisely what Critical Regionalism seeks to resist. It thus shares the doxa of the postmodern generally with respect to the end of the avant-garde, the perniciousness of Utopianism, and the fear of a universalizing homogeneity or identity. Yet its slogan of an *arrière-garde* would also seem incompatible with a postmodern "end of history" and repudiation of historical teleology, since Critical

Regionalism continues to seek a certain deeper historical logic in the past of this system, if not its future: a rearguard retains overtones of a collective resistance, and not the anarchy of trans-avant-garde pluralism that characterizes many of the postmodern ideologies of Difference as such. Meanwhile, if the current slogans of marginality and resistance are also evoked by Frampton, they would appear to carry rather different connotations than those deployed in, say, current evocations of multiculturalism, which are urban and internal First World, rather than geographically remote, as in his systematically semiperipheral examples, located in Denmark, Catalunia, Portugal, Mexico, California in the 1920s and 30s, Ticino, Japan, and Greece ("Critical Regionalism," 314–326). The enumeration warns us, to begin with, that "region" in this aesthetic program is very different from the sentimental localism we have discussed on the occasion of Buford's view of the new American short-story writers: here it designates, not a rural place that resists the nation and its power structures but rather a whole culturally coherent zone (which may also correspond to political autonomy) in tension with the stand-ardizing world system as a whole.

Such areas are not so much characterized by the emergence of strong collective identities as they are by their relative distance from the full force of global modernization, a distance that provided a shelter or an eco-niche in which regional traditions could still develop. The model shows some similari-ties to Eric Wolf's remarkable *Peasant Wars of the Twentieth Century,* which posits a relationship between remoteness from colonization and the ultimate possibility of organizing popular resistance to it. Obviously, social and collective organization has to provide a mediation in both cases: in Wolf, it is the fact that a collective or village culture was left relatively intact that enables the formation of conscious popular insurgencies (I take it that the multiculturalisms see such forms of resistance in terms of reconquest and reconstruction rather than in terms of the survival of residual traditions). Frampton quotes the Cali-fornia architect Harwell Hamilton Harris to something of the same effect:

> In California in the late Twenties and Thirties modern European ideas met a still developing regionalism. In New England, on the other hand, European Modernism met a rigid and restrictive regionalism that at first resisted and then surrendered. New England accepted European Mod-ernism whole because its own regionalism had been re-duced to a collection of restrictions.
>
> ("Critical Regionalism," 320)

It should be added, in view of Frampton's explicit dissociation of Critical Regionalism from populism (*Anti-Aesthetic,* 20–21), that this is not to be understood as a political movement as such (another feature that distinguishes it from the essentially political conception of the modernist avant-gardes). Indeed, the untheorized nature of its relationship to the social and political movements that might be expected to accompany its development, to serve as a cultural context, or to lend morale and support, is something of a problem here. What seems clear is that a mediation of intellectuals and professionals is foreseen in which these strata retain a kind of semi-autonomy: we may then conjecture a political situation in which the status of national professionals, of the local architects and engineers, is threatened by the increasing control of global technocracies and long-distance corporate decision-makers and their staffs. In such a situation, then, the matter of the survival of national intellectuals becomes itself allegorical of the politics of national autonomy as such, and the suggestion of idealism that may accompany a defense of the survival of national artistic styles is regrounded in social existence and practice.

There is thus a sense in which Critical Regionalism can be opposed both to modernism and to postmodernism alike. On the other hand, if one wished rather to stress its more fundamental vocation to resist a range of postmodern trends and temptations, Frampton offers a revised account of architectural history that would document a continuity between a certain High Modernism and the critical-regional practice of the present day:

A tectonic impulse may be traced across the century uniting diverse works irrespective of their different origins . . . Thus for all their stylistic idiosyncrasies a very similar level of tectonic articulation patently links Henrik Petrus Berlage's Stock Exchange of 1895 to Frank Lloyd Wright's Larkin Building of 1904 and Herman Hertzberger's Central Beheer office complex of 1974. In each instance there is a similar concatenation of span and support that amounts to a tectonic syntax in which gravitational force passes from purlin to truss, to pad stone, to corbel, to arch, to pediment and abutment. The technical transfer of this load passes through a series of appropriately articulated transi-

The Constraints

> tions and joints . . . We find a comparable concern for the
> revealed joint in the architecture of both Auguste Perret
> and Louis Kahn. (*Architectural Design,* 24)

We will return in a moment to the formal implications of this historical revision in which it is modernism (and in particular the work of Frank Lloyd Wright), whose essential telos is now located in a tectonic vocation.

On the other hand, with a little ingenuity, Critical Regionalism could be readjusted to its postmodern position in our scheme, on the basis of its post-Utopian disillusionment and its retreat from the overweening high modernist conception of the monument and the megastructure, and of the spatial innovation powerful enough to change the world in a genuinely revolutionary way. From this perspective, Critical Regionalism could be seen to share postmodernism's more general contextualism; as for the valorization of the part or fragment, it is a kind of thinking that here returns in an unexpected way, namely, via the synecdochic function whereby the individual building comes to stand for the local spatial culture generally. In this sense, Critical Regionalism could be characterized as a kind of postmodernism of the global system as a whole (or at least of the semiperiphery if not the Third World), as opposed to the First World's own internal and external postmodernisms that I have described earlier.

But it will be more useful, in conclusion, to sketch out the oppositions and tensions between the critical-regionalist aesthetic and the features of an actually existing postmodernism, something I propose to map according to the graph opposite.

The new schema suggests some interesting formal aspects, in addition to the logical possibilities of new lateral syntheses or combinations that are intriguing enough to be left for another time. The crucial issues to be touched on now are, however, the theme of "joints and supports" as well as that of the tectonic generally; the matter of the scenographic and also

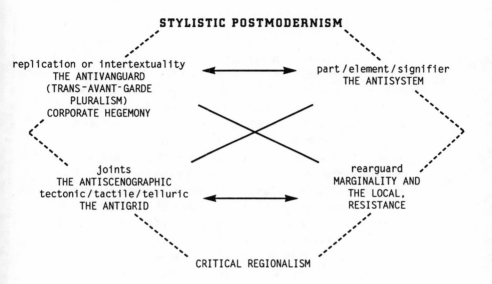

of the "grid"; and finally the role of technology in all this, or in other words of the truest bearer of modernity (if not of modernism) in the architectural process.

It is at any rate by way of form itself that the new aesthetic is best approached, for in this area Frampton provides a series of features that are systematically defined in opposition to current doxa, and in particular to Venturi's influential description of the essentials of any building in terms of the "decorated shed"—or in other words the facade with its ornament and the space that is constructed and projected behind it. Both these features are categories of the representational for Frampton, and it is indeed the very primacy of representation in contemporary architecture that the notion of a Critical Regionalism is designed fundamentally to challenge. He does not engage in any elaborate polemic with the idea of the spatial, save to observe everything that is abstract about it (when contrasted to place [*Anti-Aesthetic* 24–25]): an abstraction in the concept that itself replicates abstraction in the instrumental relationship to the world itself. Indeed, his selection of a remark by Vittorio Gregotti—"The worst enemy of modern architecture is the idea of space considered solely in terms of its economic and technical exigencies indifferent to the idea of the site"—would seem to authorize a dialectical continuation, for which a certain aesthetic abstraction of space could be grasped as the correlative to the economic and technical one evoked here. Space can indeed not be seen as such, and in that sense a "space" is difficult to theorize as an aesthetic object in its own right; yet it is perhaps because the critique of visual representation (that will come into its own in the related discussion of the facade) does not take directly on this abstract aesthetization of space, that the diagnosis of the "scenographic" is here so brilliantly proposed and deployed. Flamboyant spaces become visible as the scene of imaginary gestures and dramas, and it is by way of this supplement of the melodramatic and the theatrical that a critique of commodity form can enter the more properly architectural diagnosis (it would for example be of no little interest to prolong this analysis in the direction of Michael Fried's historical theory of modernism as a tendential resistance of "absorption" to "theatricality"). Frampton's own working philosophical categories here are "ontological" (as opposed to "representational") categories; besides invoking Heidegger's conception of the relationship of dwelling to building, he would seem to rely heavily on the more problematical (or "humanist") notion of "experience" as an alternative to the spectacle and commodity conceptions of the visual and the scenographic.

In fact, however, Frampton has a more formal alternative to these particular aesthetic modes—an alternative framed by the tripartite values of the tactile, the tectonic, and the telluric, which frame the notion of space in such a way that it turns back slowly into a conception of place once again. This alternative tends now to displace those parts of the building that are visible (and thus lend themselves to categories of the visual arts) in favor of a "privileging of the joint as the primordial tectonic element": a nonvisual and nonrepresentational category which Frampton attributes to Gottfried Semper and which for him constitutes "the fundamental nexus around which building comes into being, that is to say, comes to be articulated as a presence in itself" ("Rappel à l'ordre," 22). The category of the joint as a primal articulation of the two forces that meet in it (along with its correlative of the "'break' or 'dis-joint' . . . that point at which things break against each other rather than connect: that significant fulcrum at which one system, surface or material abruptly ends to give way to another" ("Rappel à l'ordre," 24) would seem to be the fundamental innovation of the aesthetic of Critical Regionalism, whose non- or antirepresentational equivalent for the other arts (or literature) remains to be worked out.

In my view, Frampton's more conventional emphasis on the tactile features of such buildings is best grasped by way of this more fundamentally structural one of forces in opposition, rather than as the privileging of one type of bodily sense ("touch") as opposed to another ("sight"). Indeed, his illustrations—the relationship between a solid parquet and "the momentum of an induced gait and the relative inertia of the body" in Visconti's *The Damned,* for example (*Anti-Aesthetic* 28)— would seem to authorize an interpretation whereby it is the isolation of the individual sense that becomes the fundamental symptom of postmodern alienation, an isolation most often visual, but which one could just as easily imagine in terms of tactility (as for example in the gleaming—but obviously highly tactile—surfaces of Venturi's Gordon Wu Hall, or the remarkable film of running water of Norman Foster's Century Tower in Tokyo, where paper-thin water itself becomes virtually a new and undiscovered Science-Fictional element akin to polished concrete or steel). The aesthetic of Critical Regionalism would presumably have to insist on the synaesthetic or structural-relational sensoriality of even the tactile as a vehicle for that more fundamental category and value that is the tectonic itself.

The related value of the "telluric" can also be grasped in this way, as a seemingly Heideggerian and archaic, "rear-guard" emphasis on the earth itself and on traditional sacred structures, which can also be read far more contemporaneously as a systematic negation of that emphasis on the grid (that is to say, on abstract and homogeneous corporate space) that we have found both Koolhaas and Eisenman obliged to engage in one way or another in their only partially "postmodern" forms of production. Here it is the way in which the tectonic and its fundamental category, the joint, necessarily enforces a downward distribution of pressures and forces that can be said, not merely to reveal and acknowledge the site as such but even in some creative sense to unveil and to produce it as though for the first time (Gregotti is again quoted to the effect that such "siting" constitutes "an act of knowledge of the context that comes out of its architectural modification" ("Rappel à l'ordre" 24). But at that point, the negation of the value of the grid ceases to be a merely ideological option (a kind of "humanist" preference for place over against the alienated poststructural and postmodern dehumanization of space) and expresses a positive and formal architectural value in its own right: a value that goes a long way toward "regrounding" (in all the senses of this word) Frampton's defense of the various forms of local or regional "critical" architecture in the global differentiation of the "ground" thus "marked" and "broken" by a truly telluric-tactile construction.

We must now finally come to the role of technology and modernity in this aesthetic for it is in the unique relationship of Critical Regionalism to such "Western" realities that this proposal most fundamentally distinguishes itself from the populist or cultural-nationalist, Third World, and anti-Western or antimodern responses with which we are familiar. However deliberately regressive and tradition-oriented this aesthetic may seem, insisting as it does on what Raymond Williams would have called a cultural politics of the "residual" rather than the "emergent" in the contemporary situation, it equally explicitly acknowledges the existence and the necessity of modern technology in ways whose originality must now be shown. We have already seen, for example, how Koolhaas acknowledged the constraint and "necessity" of technological modernity (that "one third of the section of a building . . . [is] inaccessible to architectural thought") by concentrating it into the single fixed point of a kind of architectural "condensor" (the 1811 Manhattan grid plan for urbanism, the elevator for the individual building) whose acceptance released the surrounding space to a new kind of freedom or innovation.

Frampton's conception of the acknowledgement of this necessity seems both less programmatic in that it does not foresee a single kind of solution to the matter the way Koolhaas seems to do, and more "philosophical" or even ideological

insofar as the dualistic nature of the opposition between technology and its other is somehow through his various examples
always maintained (this is the sense, for example, in which he
can even evoke Norman Foster's work—here the Sainsbury
center of 1978—with its "discrimination between servant and
served spaces" as an articulation still distantly redolent of
properly tectonic values ["Rappel à l'ordre," 25] rather than as
the outright "late-modern" technological and corporate celebration seen by other analysts such as Jencks).

    Still, two of his crucial illustrations for the exemplification
of an already existing Critical Regionalism would seem to
open up this dualism in a suggestively new way and to stage
this aesthetic as a strategy for somehow including and defusing
technological modernity, for outsmarting it in the very con-
structional process itself. Thus he shows how Jorn Utzon's
Bagsvaerd Church projects a kind of double life, its exterior
"combination of modular assembly and *in-situ* casting" consti-

tuting "an appropriate integration of the full range of concrete techniques which are now at our disposal" and "not only accord[ing] with the values of universal civilisation but also 'represent[ing]' its capacity for normative application" ("Critical Regionalism" 314); while the interior of the church suddenly projects a vault that goes well beyond its customary signification of "the sacred in Western culture" and indeed incorporates "the subtle and contrary allusions" deployed by the Chinese pagoda roof (along with the "Nordic vernacular of the stave church"), whose ideological consequences as an architectural "symbolic act" Frampton here analyzes with exemplary perspicuity ("Critical Regionalism" 315).

A rather different, if not inverted, way of dealing with the modern Frampton then deduces from the practice of Tadao Ando, whose very theory (itself no doubt a development out of the uniquely Japanese philosophical attention to what was in the 1930s and 1940s called the problem of "overcoming modernity") characterizes it as the strategy of an "enclosed modernity": here the technological is as it were wrapped within the renewal of more authentic Japanese attention to light and detail and thus ultimately to what Frampton calls the tectonic ("Critical Regionalism" 324). The procedure here would seem to be something like the reversal or inversion of Utzon's move, described above; yet both hold out the possibility of inventing some new relationship to the technological beyond nostalgic repudiation or mindless corporate celebration. If Critical Regionalism is to have any genuine content, it will do so only on the strength of such invention and its capacity to "enclose" or to reopen and transfigure the burden of the modern.

It is, however, worth emphasizing the degree to which the very concept and program of Critical Regionalism reflects its moment in history, and in particular expresses the pathos of a situation in which the possibility of a radical alternative to late capitalist technologies (in both architecture and urbanism alike) has decisively receded. Here not the emergent but the residual is emphasized (out of historical necessity), and the theoretical problem is at one with a political one, namely, how to fashion a progressive strategy out of what are necessarily the materials of tradition and nostalgia? How to use the attempt to conserve in an actively liberatory and transformational way? The problem has its historical roots in the specificity of postmodern technology and urbanism, where "progress"—if the concept exists at all any longer—involves a very different ratio of the introduction of new machinery to the transformation of the built environment than it did in the nineteenth century (in which a different kind of technology obtained, with a very different, more visible and stylistic impact on nature than is the case with the information technologies). So it is that today very often some of the most militant urban or neighborhood movements draw their vitality from the attempt to prevent an older city fabric from being disaggregated or destroyed altogether: something that foretells significant and ominous dilemmas in coordinating such "chains of equivalence" (to speak like Laclau and Mouffe again) with those of "new social movements" that necessarily refuse such conservative family-and-neighborhood ideological motivations.

Frampton's conceptual proposal, however, is not an internal but rather a geopolitical one: it seeks to mobilize a pluralism of "regional" styles (a term selected, no doubt, in order to forestall the unwanted connotations of the terms *national* and *international* alike), with a view toward resisting the standardizations of a henceforth global late capitalism and corporatism, whose "vernacular" is as omnipresent as its power over local decisions (and indeed, after the end of the Cold War, over local governments and individual nation states as well).

It is thus politically important, returning to the problem of parts or components, to emphasize the degree to which the concept of Critical Regionalism is necessarily allegorical. What the individual buildings are henceforth here a unit of is no longer a unique vision of city planning (such as the Baroque) nor a specific city fabric (like Las Vegas) but rather a distinctive regional culture as a whole, for which the distinctive individual building becomes a metonym. The construction of such a building resembles the two previously discussed movements of a stylistic postmodernism and Italian neorationalism to the degree to which it must also deploy a storehouse of preexisting forms and traditional motifs, as signs and markers by which to "decorate" what generally remains a relatively conventional Western "shed."

In order for this kind of building to make a different kind of statement, its decorations must also be grasped as recognizable elements in a cultural-national discourse, and the building of the building must be grasped at one and the same time as a physical structure and as a symbolic act that reaffirms the regional-national culture as a collective possibility in its moment of besiegement and crisis. But perhaps it is with allegory as with the mythical that its effects remain wanting unless the object has been labeled in advance and we have been told beforehand that it is an allegorical effect that has been sought after? This interesting theoretical problem, how-ever, becomes visible only when a "text" is isolated from the social ground in which its effects are generated: in the present instance, for example, it should be clear enough that an archi-tectural form of Critical Regionalism would lack all political and allegorical efficacy unless it were coordinated with a vari-ety of other local, social, and cultural movements that aimed at securing national autonomy. It was one of the signal errors of the artistic activism of the 1960s to suppose that there existed, in advance, forms that were in and of themselves endowed with a political, and even revolutionary, potential by virtue of their own intrinsic properties. On the other hand, there remains a danger of idealism implicit in all forms of cultural nationalism as such, which tends to overestimate the effectivity of culture and consciousness and to neglect the concomitant requirement of economic autonomy. But it is precisely economic autonomy that has been everywhere called back into question in the postmodernity of a genuinely global late capitalism.

An even graver objection to the strategies of Critical Regionalism, as to the various postmodernisms generally when they claim a political vocation for themselves, is awakened by the value of pluralism and the slogan of difference they all in one way or another endorse. The objection does not consist in some conviction that pluralism is always a liberal, rather than a truly radical, value—a dogmatic and doctrinaire position that the examination of any number of active moments of history would be enough to dispel. No, the uneasiness stems from the very nature of late capitalism itself, about which it can be wondered whether pluralism and difference are not somehow related to its own deeper internal dynamics.

It is a feeling raised, for example, by the new strategies of what is now called post-Fordism: the term can be seen as one of the optional variants for such terms as *postmodernity* or *late capitalism,* with which it is roughly synonymous. However, it underscores one of the originalities of multinational capitalism today in a way that tends to problematize the assumptions of the strategy of critical regionalism itself. Where Fordism and classical imperialism, in other words, designed their products centrally and then imposed them by fiat on an emergent public (you do have a choice of color with the Model-T: Black!), post-Fordism puts the new computerized technology to work by custom-designing its products for individual markets. This has indeed been called postmodern marketing, and it can be thought to "respect" the values and cultures of the local population by adapting its various goods to suit those vernacular languages and practices. Unfortunately this inserts the corporations into the very heart of local and regional culture, about which it becomes difficult to decide whether it is authentic any longer (and indeed whether that term still means anything). It is the EPCOT syndrome raised to a global scale and returns us to the question of the "critical" with a vengeance, since now the "regional" as such becomes the business of global American Disneyland-related corporations, who will redo your own native architecture for you more exactly than you can do it yourself. Is global Difference the same today as global Identity?

Bibliography

Attali, Jacques. *Noise*. Minneapolis: University of Minnesota Press, 1985.

Borie, Jean. *Le Célibataire français*. Paris: Le Sagittaire, 1976.

Brodsky, Joseph. "Catastrophes in the Air." In *Less than One*. New York: Farrar, Strauss, Giroux, 1986.

Buford, Bill. Introduction to "New American Writing." *Granta*, no. 8. (1983).

Burger, Peter. *Theory of the Avant-Garde*. Minneapolis: University of Minnesota Press, 1984.

Claudel, Paul. Preface to Arthur Rimbaud. *Oeuvres complètes*. Paris: Mercure de France, 1912.

Colletti, Lucio. *Marxism and Hegel*. London: Verso, 1973.

Collingwood, R. G. *Essay on Metaphysics*. Oxford: Oxford University Press, 1940.

Deleuze, Gilles. *Présentation de Sacher-Masoch*. Paris: Editions de Minuit, 1967.

Eisenman, Peter. *House X*. New York: Rizzoli, 1982.

———. *Moving Arrows, Eros, and Other Errors: An Architecture of Absence*. London: Architectural Association, 1986.

———. *Recent Projects.* Edited by Arie Graafland. Nijmegen: Idea Books, 1989.

———. *El Croquis.* Special Issue no. 41 (October/December 1989).

Elliott, Robert C. *The Shape of Utopia.* Chicago: University of Chicago Press, 1970.

FitzGerald, Frances. *Fire in the Lake.* Boston: Little, Brown, 1972.

Flatley, Jonathan. "Platonov's Melancholy Bodies: Mourning, Utopia, and Sexuality in *Chevengur.*" Annual Bulletin, Institute of Philosophy of the Russian Academy of Sciences, Moscow. Forthcoming.

Frampton, Kenneth. "Towards a Critical Regionalism: Six Points for an Architecture of Resistance." In Hal Foster, ed., *The Anti-Aesthetic.* Seattle: Bay Press, 1983.

———. "Critical Regionalism: Modern Architecture and Cultural Identity." In K. Frampton, *Modern Architecture: A Critical History.* London: Thames and Hudson, 1985.

———. "Rappel à l'ordre: The Case for the Tectonic." *Architectural Design* 50, no. 3/4 (1991).

Freud, Sigmund. "The Antithetical Meaning of Primal Words." *The Standard Edition,* vol. 11, pp. 153–161. London: The Hogarth Press, 1957.

Fuss, Diana. *Essentially Speaking.* London: Routledge, 1989.

Groys, Boris. *Gesamtkunstwerk Stalin.* Munich: Hanser, 1988.

Guha, Ranajit. *A Rule of Property for Bengal.* Paris and The Hague: Mouton, 1963.

Habermas, Jurgen and Niklas Luhmann. *Theorie der Gesellschaft oder Sozialtechnologie.* Frankfurt: Suhrkamp, 1971.

Hindess, Barry and Paul Hirst, A. Cutler, and A. Hussein. *Marx's Capital and Capitalism Today.* 2 vols. London: Routledge and Kegan Paul, 1977.

Hirschman, Albert O. *The Passions and the Interests.* Princeton: Princeton University Press, 1977.

Huntington, Samuel. "Political Order and Political Decay." In S. Huntington, ed., *Political Order in Changing Societies.* New Haven: Yale University Press, 1968.

Jacobs, Jane. *The Death and Life of Great American Cities.* New York: Random House, 1961.

Jameson, Fredric. *Late Marxism.* London: Verso, 1992.

———. *Postmodernism; or, The Cultural Logic of Late Capitalism.* Durham: Duke University Press, 1992.

————. "World Reduction in Le Guin." *Science Fiction Studies* 2, no. 3 (1975).

Kant, Immanuel. *The Critique of Pure Reason.* 1781. Reprint, London: Macmillan, 1958.

Karatani, Kojin. *The Origins of Modern Japanese Literature.* Durham: Duke University Press, 1992.

Kojève, Alexandre. *Introduction à la lecture de Hegel.* Paris: Gallimard, 1947.

Koolhaas, Rem. *Delirious New York.* New York: Oxford University Press, 1978.

————. Interview in *El Croquis.* Special issue, vol. 53 (Madrid) (March 1992).

Laclau, Ernesto and Chantal Mouffe. *Hegemony and Socialist Strategy.* London: Verso, 1985.

Lefaivre, Liane. "Dirty Realism in European Architecture Today." *Design Book Review* 17 (Winter 1989): 17–20.

Lefebvre, Henri. *The Production of Space.* Oxford: Blackwell, 1991.

Lévi-Strauss, Claude. *La geste d'Asdiwal.* Paris: Imprimerie Nationale, 1958.

Lippard, Lucy. *Overlay.* New York: Pantheon, 1983.

Loos, Adolf. "Ornament and Crime." In L. Münz and G. Küntsler, *Adolf Loos: Pioneer of Modern Architecture.* London: Thames and Hudson, 1966.

Macherey, Pierre. *A Theory of Literary Production.* London: Routledge and Kegan Paul, 1978.

Marcuse, Herbert. "On the Affirmative Character of Culture." In *Negations,* trans. by Jeremy J. Shapiro. Boston: Beacon Press, 1968.

Mayer, Arno. *The Persistence of the Old Regime.* New York: Pantheon, 1981.

Podoroga, Valery. "The Eunuch of the Soul: Positions of Reading and the World of Platonov." *SAQ* 90, no. 2 (Spring 1991): 357–408.

Proust, Marcel. *A la recherche du temps perdu.* 4 vols. Paris: Bibliothèque de la Pléiade, 1987–1989.

Rey, Pierre-Philippe. *Les alliances de classes.* Paris: Maspero, 1973.

Robinson, Kim Stanley. *Red Mars.* New York: Bantam, 1993.

Rorty, Richard. *Philosophy and the Mirror of Nature.* Princeton: Princeton University Press, 1980.

Smith, Paul. *Discerning the Subject.* Minneapolis: University of Minnesota Press, 1988.

Tafuri, Manfredo. *Architecture and Utopia*. Cambridge: MIT Press, 1976.

Thompson, E. P. "Time, Work-Discipline, and Industrial Capitalism." *Past and Present,* vol. 38 (December 1967).

Venturi, Robert, Denise Scott Brown, and Steven Izenour. *Learning from Las Vegas*. Cambridge: MIT Press, 1977.

Virilio, Paul. *War and Cinema*. London: Verso, 1989.

Wolf, Eric. *Peasant Wars of the Twentieth Century*. New York: Harper and Row, 1969.

van Wolferén, Karel. *The Enigma of Japanese Power*. New York: Knopf, 1989.

Yakushev, Henryka. "Andrei Platonov's Artistic Model of the World." *Russian Literature Triquarterly* 16 (1979): 171–188.

Index

Adorno, T. W., 13, 40, 47, 189
Albee, Edward, 175
Althusser, Louis, 3, 16, 135, 167, 174
Ando, Tadao, 201
Arendt, Hannah, 154
Aristotle, 33, 36
Attali, Jacques, 76

Bakhtin, Mikhail, 23, 31, 108
Ballard, J. G., 176
Blazac, Honoré de, 153
Barthes, Roland, 16, 37, 180
Bataille, Georges, 24
Baudelaire, Charles, 12, 84, 86
Beauvoir, Simone de, 34
Benjamin, Walter, 184
Bergson, Henri, 8
Blade Runner (Ridley Scott, 1982), 146, 150, 155, 157

Bloch, Ernst, 79
Borie, Jean, 37
Brecht, Bertolt, 152
Buford, Bill, 145–150, 191
Bürger, Peter, 189
Burke, Edmund, 31, 51

Chandler, Raymond, 158
Claudel, Paul, 89
Coletti, Lucio, 2–3
Collingwood, R. G., 37–39
Confucius, 20, 49, 125
Critical Regionalism, 184, 189–204

Delany, Samuel R., 28
Deleuze, Gilles, 10, 22, 41, 55, 138
de Man, Paul, 3, 184
Derrida, Jacques, 23, 38, 167

Descartes, Réné, 51
Dewey, John, 38
Dickens, Charles, 153

Eagleton, Terry, 167–169
Einstein, Albert, 69
Eisenman, Peter, 142, 162–183, 185, 188, 198
Engels, Friedrich, 15

Fanon, Frantz, 34
FitzGerald, Frances, 125
Flaubert, Gustave, 35, 37, 84, 160
Ford, Henry, 40, 204
Forster, E. M., 115
Foster, Norman, 198, 200
Foucault, Michel, 34
Fourier, Charles, 55, 57, 58–59, 65
Frampton, Kenneth, 175, 184, 189–204
Freud, Sigmund, 4, 7, 13, 75, 169
Fried, Michael, 197
Fuss, Diana, 45

Galileo Galilei, 77
Gehry, Frank, 144, 145, 157
Gibson, William, 155
Gide, André, xv
Gramsci, Antonio, 65
Graves, Michael, 164, 185
Gregotti, Vittorio, 196, 198
Greimas, A. J., xiii
Groys, Boris, 31, 51
Guha, Ranajit, 24

Habermas, Jürgen, 43, 80
Haraway, Donna, 138

Harris, Harwell Hamilton, 192
Hegel, G. W. F., xvi, 5, 6, 7, 13, 18, 131, 143, 155, 156
Heidegger, Martin, 34, 38, 77–78, 81, 85, 86, 89, 110, 197, 198
Hemingway, Ernest, 115
Hindess, Barry, and Paul Hirst, 187–188
Hirschman, A. O., 51
Holland, Norman, 174
Hugo, Victor, 153
Huntington, Samuel, 49

Jacobs, Jane, 30
Jencks, Charles, 164, 200
Joyce, James, 54, 132, 138
Jünger, Ernst, 78

Kafka, Franz, 58, 79, 123–128
Kahn, Louis, 186
Kant, Immanuel, xvi, 2, 6, 8, 15, 16, 38, 39, 42, 51
Karatani Kojin, 22
Kepler, Johannes, 77
Keynes, John Maynard, 14
Kirkpatrick, Jeanne, 48
Kojève, Alexandre, 18, 156
Koolhaas, Rem, 57–58, 60, 134–145, 164, 180, 183, 185, 188, 198, 199

Laclau, Ernesto, 43, 65, 187–188, 202
Lawrence, D. H., 164
le Carré, John, 159
Le Corbusier (Charles-Edouard Jeanneret), 54, 135, 137, 144, 146, 153

Lefaivre, Liane, 145, 150, 189
Lefebvre, Henri, 22
Le Guin, Ursula, 28
Lévi-Strauss, Claude, 3, 23–24, 86
Lippard, Lucy, 174–175
Loos, Adolf, 6, 31
Luhmann, Niklas, 80
Lukács, Georg, 36, 43–44, 120
Lynch, David, 161
Lyotard, Jean-François, 7, 35, 43, 44

Macherey, Pierre, 167–169
Mallarmé, Stéphane, 36, 54, 159–162
Mandelbrot, Benoit, 181
Mann, Thomas, 174
Marcuse, Herbert, 124
Marin, Louis, 70
Marx, Karl, 2, 4, 13, 18, 27, 29, 47, 58–59, 62, 66, 69, 75, 83, 155
Mayer, Arno, 13, 39
Mies van der Rohe, Ludwig, 36, 132, 160
Moneo, Rafael, 180
Moore, Charles, 164, 185–186
Morris, William, 55, 74
Mouffe, Chantal, 43, 65, 187–188, 202

Nabokov, Vladimir, 147
Newton, Isaac, 69
Nietzsche, Friedrich, 13, 35, 38, 184

Orwell, George, 55, 58

Parmenides, 16, 19
Platonov, Andrei, xvi–xvii, 78–82, 111–113, 119–122
Proust, Marcel, 9, 12, 21, 132

Rey, Pierre-Philippe, 26
Ricoeur, Paul, 13
Rimbaud, Arthur, 89
Robinson, Kim Stanley, 65
Rorty, Richard, 33, 38–39, 44, 51
Rossi, Aldo, 186–187
Rousseau, Jean-Jacques, 67, 126
Runge, Philipp Otto, 22
Russell, Bertrand, 182

Sartre, Jean-Paul, 12, 33–34, 37, 40, 42–43, 61, 64
Schlegel, Friedrich, 184
Schoenberg, Arnold, 132, 181
Semper, Gottfried, 197
Smith, Paul, 45
Solzhenitsyn, Aleksander, xvii
Spinoza, Baruch, 69

Tafuri, Manfredo, 13–14, 40
Thompson, E. P., 84
Tolstoy, Leo, 70
Tzonis, Alexander, 189

Utzon, Jorn, 200–201

Valéry, Paul, 8, 58
Venturi, Robert, 135, 141–143, 146, 180, 183, 185, 186, 198
Villiers de l'Isle Adam, Auguste, 9
Virilio, Paul, 9–10
Visconti, Luchino, 198

Wagner, Richard, 132, 159
Wallerstein, Immanuel, 76
Weber, Max, 23, 84–85
Wells, H. G., 55
Wilde, Oscar, 54
Williams, Raymond, 28, 70, 181, 199
Wittgenstein, Ludwig, 6, 38

Wolf, Eric, 192
Wolferén, Karel van, 158
Wright, Frank Lloyd, 132, 153, 194

Yeats, William Butler, 39

Žižek, Slavoj, 4, 76

p. 136: Rem Koolhaas, La Bibliothèque de France
(Office for Metropolitan Architecture)

p. 137: Rem Koolhaas, La Bibliothèque de France
(Office for Metropolitan Architecture)

p. 139: Rem Koolhaas, Zeebrugge Sea Terminal
(Office for Metropolitan Architecture)

p. 140: Rem Koolhaas, Zeebrugge Sea Terminal
(Office for Metropolitan Architecture)

p. 156: *Blade Runner*
(Jerry Ohlinger's Movie Materials)

pp. 170–73: Peter Eisenman, University Art
Museum, California State University at Long Beach
(Eisenman Architects)

pp. 175–78: Peter Eisenman, *Moving Arrows, Eros,
and Other Errors* (Romeo and Juliet project)
(Eisenman Architects)

p. 179: Peter Eisenman, Wexner Center for the
Arts, Ohio State University, Columbus
(Eisenman Architects; photo Wolfgang Hoyt)

p. 191: Tadao Ando, Temple under Water,
Tsuna-gun, Hyogo, Japan (Tadao Ando)

p. 200: Tadao Ando, Church of the Light,
Osaka, Japan (Tadao Ando)

Designer: Teresa Bonner
Text: Perpetua
Compositor: Maple-Vail
Printer: Maple-Vail
Binder: Maple-Vail